CONTENTS

Acknowledgments

This book has its beginning several years ago in conversations I had with Os Guinness and John Seel. I would like to thank them for their encouragement and enthusiasm—though they didn't know what would come out of it. Richard Mouw, Robert Banks, and Paul Stevens have taught me about the meaning of creation. The writings of Al Wolters on this theme have always inspired and, I think, shaped me. Mike Starkey's writings have shown me a little of what this means in some areas of life, and I will not soon forget the fashion show he put on in Doug and Ann Holt's church in London. I thank James and Wanda Coffey-Bailey, two people to whom I felt I could entrust the manuscript in its early stages: I thank them for their positive response. Ed Knipper's paintings have also shaped this book, and he and Diane Knipper's advice, encouragement, and hospitality were invaluable and much enjoyed. Howard and Robert Ahmanson have worked with these issues for many years: I hope they like what many passionate and delightful conversations with them have wrought.

If there is one person who has most shaped what I say here, it is my longtime colleague, mentor, and squash partner, Calvin Seerveld. I'm not sure if he will like all of what is here, but he is responsible for most of what is good here. The Institute for Christian Studies, at which I taught until very recently, provided an academic home and intellectually demanding environment. Last, but certainly not least, I want to thank Lela Gilbert, whose idea this book was, and who made it possible for me to write it.

——— 🐟 ———

. . . We must come to a place where we comfortably think of God as a reality that is a part of our world. Until the church develops an understanding of the gospel that relates it more to this life than the next life, it will cause difficulties on both sides. Those on the outside of religion will look at it and regard it has having nothing to do with real life. Those on the inside of religion will experience their life outside of special religious activities as if it were a godless world. I think the key issue here lies deeper than even matters of integration as we commonly discuss it. It is a matter of our understanding of the gospel of Jesus Christ as one which breaks through the natural world and brings in the spiritual world and invites us as individuals to learn to live an eternal kind of life now.

—Dallas Willard

PREFACE

You should know up front that this book is one-sided. The Bible portrays our world as *good,* destined for reunion with God in Jesus Christ. It is this *goodness* that I'll focus on here, and I make no apology for it. But the Bible also emphasizes the effects of sin on the world, and hence, creation's transitory character. Scripture teaches that God loves the world and cares for it (and always will), but also that we are sojourners in the present age. Here I have given much less attention to the second than the first.

This one-sidedness is quite deliberate. Unfortunately, among Christian believers, and especially among evangelicals, the theme of the goodness and permanence of the world is usually neglected, often forgotten, and sometimes denied entirely. Instead we are deluged with articles, books, sermons, and radio and TV programs warning us that the world, along with every human achievement, is going to be destroyed. This extreme position diminishes our place in God's world. Because of such misconceptions, many Christians today are, by and large, shirking their divinely given responsibility to sustain, nurture, renew, and really *live* in God's world.

Throughout the text are descriptive "snapshots" intended to give some glimpses of the wonders of living in God's creation. Although all of the stories are true, I have changed the names of most of the characters for the sake of privacy and protection.

This book is merely an attempt to give a brief overview of our *spiritual orientation* as we live as God's people in God's world. It gives few practical guidelines. There are no keys or twelve-step programs here. There is, however, a deep and heartfelt appeal that I hope will challenge what we think and believe about the world. The gospel calls for it. The Church needs it. And our world is literally dying for it.

This is my Father's world,
O let me ne'er forget
That though the wrong seems oft so strong,
God is the ruler yet.
This is my Father's world:
The battle is not done;
Jesus who died shall be satisfied,
And earth and heav'n be one.
—Maltbie D. Babcock

OUR FEAR
OF THE WORLD

PART I

one

THE CHURCH: A BORING GOSPEL?

Every evening the cathedral drew us like a magnet. After days in the lecture hall studying human rights law, we would amble into the city center. Brazilian lawyers, Spanish diplomats, Vietnamese foreign ministry officials, and American students chattered happily along the way, rehashing the arguments of the day or contemplating Strasbourg's gastronomic offerings.

After dinner we'd gather in the square and argue some more. The buildings round about were jewels, half-timbered and lead-glazed. They placed us in another world. Above all, stretching to the sky over our heads, was the cathedral.

A glance across the cobbled square revealed apostles and saints and angels, immortalized in stone, gazing silently back. And due to the Gothic architecture, our eyes were lifted upward, drawn irresistibly higher, past the ascending ranks of God's servants until our gaze was elevated to the spire reaching, floodlit, into the dark night.

We might not have believed what the builders believed. We might have thought that they were wasting their time in a futile enterprise. We might have assumed that their money and their skills could have been better spent otherwise. But there was no escaping their overpowering legacy. The cathedral bore mute testimony, not only to them but, vastly more important, to God. Without such faith the project could never even have begun.

Those serried ranks of stone witnesses continue to point silently and overwhelmingly to a God above, who looks down at all our doings. They do not mock modern pretensions as much as simply ignore them, offering silent stone tribute to something far greater.

During our time in Strasbourg, the carved saints' wordless witness called us to live, to work, and to rejoice in their presence. They also intimated, even to the hearts of unbelievers, that they knew of something far beyond the reaches of our human reason and understanding.

I became a Christian at a Billy Graham Crusade in England in the mid-60s. In 1968, I hitched a ride from Liverpool, my hometown, to the Swiss community of L'Abri. I had some questions for Francis Schaeffer, but I never asked most of them. When the opportunity came to ask, I couldn't formulate my questions: they were nothing more than vaguely uneasy wonderings, hovering at the ungraspable margins of thought.

JUST WHAT IS A CHRISTIAN ANYWAY?

I had a pervasive sense of guilt. I wanted to live a committed Christian life and knew that this involved holy living, evangelism, prayer, and Bible (and other) study. I also knew, or thought I knew, that there was more than this to being a Christian.

As a geology student, I wondered how my faith should relate to my studies. Of course I had questions about Genesis, geology, and evolution. But what about what we actually studied—rocks, fossils, mountains, oceans, or the earth itself? Should I be really interested in them *for their own sake?* If so, why? How much? And how on earth did this relate to the gospel?

I was also concerned about how to integrate my faith during my free time. Since I grew up in Liverpool, my one fleeting claim to fame is that I went to school with George Harrison and Paul McCartney. (John Lennon was next door at the Art College.) I was surrounded by rock music. Some was crude, but much of it I loved. Since I was now a Christian, I wondered how I was supposed to judge this, or any other, music. Was I only supposed to sing hymns? What about reading? Were novels a waste of time? What about almost anything that went on outside the life of the church?

Then there was the whole issue of sports. A central fact of life in that grimy city was, and is, football (what Americans call soccer). At that time, Liverpool reigned as the football capital of England and reached for the title of Europe as well as the rest of the world. I used to go to most games. But I didn't know whether sports should occupy so much of my time and attention.

At first I played it safe by concentrating solely on duties more apparently pious and spiritual. As long as I did, my conscience felt clear. But at the same time, I felt narrow, cramped, and frustrated—hemmed in by walls and isolated from much of the world in which I lived. On the other hand, if I delved more into study, or music, or sports, or any other facet of human life, then my heart was freer and I was happier, but my conscience pricked me. I worried about the effects of such "worldly" pursuits on my Christian life. These activities didn't (usually) involve evangelism. They didn't involve prayer. How could I justify them? It wasn't that I was involved in anything inherently sinful: the question was why be involved in anything at all? The Apostle Paul said, "If the trumpet gives an uncertain sound, who can prepare for the battle?" (1 Cor. 14:8). For what battle was I preparing? I wasn't sure. There was just a vague sense of restlessness, of unease. I didn't know my place in the world, and to make matters worse, I didn't *know* that I didn't know.

One thing, however, was abundantly clear. Despite my primitive theological understanding, the gospel was daily and consistently expanding my horizons and feeding my curiosity. I became interested in how this life-giving message could be integrated with work, philosophy, and society. I even developed an interest in people (though this took a long time, since I am English).

At university, I faced the usual questions about whether, if I was a committed Christian, I shouldn't be going into "full-time" Christian ministry. Eventually I concluded that I shouldn't, since I had few of the necessary skills, and anyway the whole idea terrified me (as it would have terrified any congregation or mission field unfortunate enough to have had me). But, then, what did it mean to live a reasonably whole, integrated, and committed Christian life?

WHY ARE WE HERE?

At L'Abri I hadn't known what questions to ask, so I never asked them. But the questions never disappeared. In the decades since, a large part of my life has been a struggle to learn how all these dimensions of human life should fit together. I've met many guides, both in person and, more usually, through their writings. The greatest guides were often long dead. They showed that throughout much of its history, the Church has had a unique vision of both the fullness of human life and the goodness of creation. That is why the gospel has always shaped our world.

Yet in the modern world, one crippling problem we face as Christians—particularly, as evangelical Christians—is that we don't quite know *why we're here.* We're not too sure what we're supposed to be doing with our lives.

At first glance, these seem like silly statements—surely we know who we are. We are God's children. We are saved by Jesus Christ. We are called to proclaim him to all people as our Lord and Savior, and theirs. Isn't that enough?

We have sermons, books, manuals, lectures, tapes, and videos on evangelism, prayer, bible study, and the role and function of the local church. There are guides for everything, from marriage and parenting to maintaining physical and emotional health. There are guides to help us work more efficiently and to better understand industry, education, and society. There are even works calling us to appreciate the arts and literature. Many of these resources are very good. Yet few of them answer one vital question: how do any of these things relate to the God-given pupose of our life?

In some ways we have too many guides and too much advice. We can learn—or pretend to learn—how to speak, pray, sing, share, study, read, make music, raise children, change legislation, recycle, give money, make money, save money, start churches, build churches, split churches, vote, be intimate, play, lobby, demonstrate, join neighborhoods, organize neighborhoods, leave neighborhoods, overcome workaholism, or become workaholics.

But still there's a problem, a massive one. If we don't know why we are here, how can we learn how all these parts fit together? How can we have an overall vision of Christian service? How do all the facets of our lives connect with the kingdom of God, to Jesus' life, death, and resurrection? Because we often don't know, many of us live with an uneasy conscience. We live in, rejoice in, and reshape the world, but we're not sure why.

WHEN LIGHT LEAVES, DARKNESS FOLLOWS

Often our theology seems to tell us one thing and our heart tells us another. A tension tugs our mind when our heart goes one way, or tugs our heart when our mind goes the other. It's either quiet guilt or quiet frustration. How can we party when we might be praying? How can we spend money on movies that could go to missions? Unless these are things we *ought* to do rather than *can* do, why give them any place at all?

One result is that we become half-hearted (or half-minded or half-bodied) people. We become timid, cautious, and guarded. The evangelical "taboos" that once distinguished us from the rest of the world—don't drink, don't dance, don't go to movies—have slowly died out. Perhaps this is in response to Paul's teachings in Colossians, which caution against restrictions "based on human commands and teachings" that are "destined to perish" (Col. 2:20–22). Yet, as the Christian subculture becomes less and less distinct, it has less impact on culture and society as a whole.

The United States is unusual and remarkable among industrialized countries because of the number of people who claim to be Christians. Over half of America goes to church regularly, and many attend evangelical churches. Yet in much of our society, Christian beliefs and values are conspicuously absent. If we watch network TV or movies, read newspapers and magazines, or go to university or the theater, it's as if the gospel does not exist or exists only as something alien and evil. Why?

One reason is that, among those who actually teach at major universities, work in network television or in movies, write for major newspapers, or are otherwise involved in the media, the percentage of committed believers seems to be only about 3 percent. The major patterns of our culture and society are being shaped with almost no Christian presence. We live in a "subculture," on our own island, increasingly far from shore.

And when we do seek influence, we often only react to someone else's proposals. If the Disney Company puts out movies that trivialize or demonize the Christian faith, we boycott them. But this simply pulls us farther into our own shell. We have no alternative to put forward, no movies that undercut Disney because they're better. A familiar proverb says, "The fool curses the darkness, but the wise man lights a candle." We "curse" a lot but have few candles, and so the darkness deepens.

"NICE" CHRISTIANS

If we are ever going to change this trend and become a vital part of our world, we must begin to demonstrate that there is something vital and life-changing about Christianity. So much of

Christian faith today is "nice." Cautious. Pleasant. Cheerful. Often if we are interesting to non-Christians at all, it is not because of our faith, but *in spite of it*. Christianity puts most people (often including ourselves) to sleep.

We have only to look at the example of our Lord to know that this is not the way our faith is to be lived. Whatever else Jesus was, and he was many things, he was never, ever "nice." (The term *nice* originally meant silly or stupid.[1]) And he certainly wasn't boring. As Dorothy Sayers said:

The people who hanged Christ never, to do them justice, accused Him of being a bore; on the contrary, they thought Him too dynamic to be safe. It has been left for later generations to muffle up that shattering personality and surround Him with an atmosphere of tedium. We have very efficiently pared the claws of the Lion of Judah, certified Him "meek and mild," and recommended Him as a fitting household pet for pale curates and pious old ladies.

To those who knew Him, however, He in no way suggested a milk-and-water person; they objected to Him as a dangerous firebrand. True, He was tender to the unfortunate, patient with honest inquirers, and humble before Heaven; but He insulted respectable clergymen by calling them hypocrites, He referred to King Herod as "that fox"; He went to parties in disreputable company and was looked upon as a "gluttonous man and a wine-bibber, a friend of publicans and sinners"; He assaulted indignant tradesmen and threw them and their belongings out of the Temple; He drove a coach-and-horses through a number of sacrosanct and hoary regulations; He cured diseases by any means that came handy, with a shocking casualness in the matter

*of other people's pigs and property; He showed no proper defer-
ence for wealth or social position.*[2]

Of course most of us are a lot better than guilty, half-hearted, and boring. But many of our versions of the Christian faith push us in that direction. Often we spend our time trying passively to avoid sin rather than trying positively to do good. This, too, makes us live tentatively, cautiously. So as not to break a rule, we play it safe and do not much of anything.

THE IMPORTANCE OF GOD'S WORLD

There are doubtless many reasons for our passivity, but one crucial one is that we don't take God's world seriously. We have accepted the heretical idea that the body will pass permanently away after death, and that we will only reappear as some type of disembodied wraith.[3] But the Bible will have none of this. When Jesus rose from the dead, he had fish for lunch and overcame the despair of doubting Thomas by telling him to put his finger in his all-too-fleshly wounds. The creeds of the Christian Church universally affirm, *"I believe in the resurrection of the body."*

It is also an unbiblical idea that the earth doesn't matter because we are going to go to heaven when we die. The Bible teaches that there will be *"a new heaven and a new earth."* Our destiny is an earthly one: a new earth, an earth redeemed and transfigured. An earth reunited with heaven, but an earth, nevertheless.

If we think that the earth and everything on it is simply going to disappear, why labor long and hard to write something, perform something, build something, create something that will only be consumed by fire? If we think that being human is only a passing and trivial phase of life, why take the present seriously? Why not regard ourselves merely as apprentice angels, stuck for the moment in an earthly waiting room but better suited to and anxiously awaiting life on some disembodied, heavenly plane?

The truth, however, is that we are embodied, earthly creatures made in God's image. And if we are really to begin to live in God's world, we need to see what the Bible actually says about the goodness of the creation and the purpose of human life. To do this, we should begin where the Bible itself does, in the book of Genesis.

OUR PLACE
IN THE WORLD

PART II

two

C REATION AND RESPONSIBILITY

Off the east coast of Borneo lies the isle of Sipadan, nestled in deep blue water, carpeted in palms, fringed with beaches and coral reefs, and nearly unspoiled by human beings. Along the shoreline giant turtles still come to lay their eggs, and enormous coconut crabs climb the trees. Thirty feet offshore, the white sand drops away in a sheer cliff to the ocean floor two thousand feet below. And off the southern tip of this marine paradise, the tidal currents create a slow, lazy whirlpool.

For reasons known only to them, thousands of barracuda gather here. They too drift in a slow, lazy swirl, spiraling up a hundred feet to the water's surface. They don't seem to mind if you swim through their fishy barrier into the vortex, to immerse yourself in a world of metallic gray, sharp-toothed predators.

We entered this whirlpool seventy feet down and gazed at the surface far above, at the center of the quivering spiral. As the sun reflected off the silver-finned walls, we slowly rose up toward the light. Our fear was overcome by our sense of wonderment, even rapture. Barracuda have a fearsome reputation and an even more fearsome look, but they paid us no heed as they circled. We were overcome by the sheer joy of being alive, overawed that a world such as this could be—a world suffused with splendor and magic, a world beyond our imagining.

I knew then, more deeply than ever before, that this world is a gift from God, a treasure to be cared for, honored, experienced, and lived in. It is no passing fancy to be discarded when the drama of salvation is complete. It is God's world, our home.

DID GOD MAKE US?

For Christians, the question "Why are we here?" is instead "Why did God make us?" The Bible starts with this question in the story of creation given in the book of beginnings, Genesis (1:1–2:3). Here the Bible tells us what it means to be man and woman in God's world. It tells us why God made the world, and why he made us.

In Genesis 1:28 God says to the first man and woman: "Be fruitful and increase in number, and fill the earth, and subdue it. Rule over the fish of the seas and the birds of the air and over every living creature that moves on the ground." God's command to them, and through them to all of us, comes as the finale and climax of the entire story of creation. Genesis opens with the declaration that in the beginning God created both the heavens and the earth. Then, through eight creative words, we are shown how God made our wonderful world out of that which was, at first, "without form and void."

On the first day darkness is separated from light, night from day (vv. 3–5).

On the second day the waters above and below are separated (vv. 6–8).

On the third day the lower waters are divided into dry land and sea, and then the land is filled with vegetation (vv. 9–12).

On the fourth day God makes the heavenly lights appear: sun, moon, and stars (vv.14–19).

On the fifth day God fills the air and sea with birds and fishes (vv. 20–22).

This description of God's acts on the first five days is not random, as if God simply got up each morning and decided to try something new. The story shows a careful and definite progression as God works and shapes like a master craftsman, gradually building and forming the earth as he had planned from the beginning. One task follows another and builds on it. Hence, what God does on the sixth day is not merely the last act on his list. Rather, it points to the *culmination* of God's purpose. It is God's finishing touch.

God's actions on the sixth and seventh days tell us what the whole creation is about. On the sixth day God first creates the animals (vv. 24–25), and then the man and woman. Having made this human couple, God says to them, *as the very last act in the drama of creation,* that they must "be fruitful" and rule over creation.

God's command is presented as the climax of the creation story: once it is given, the creation of the world is complete. After the man and woman are told what God wants them to do then God's work is, for a time, concluded. He pronounces it good, and he rests (2:1–2).

CREATED TO HAVE DOMINION

When we say that Adam and Eve were given their task, even the words *instruction* or *command* are far too weak to convey the depth of what is happening. The emphasis at this point in Genesis is not so much what God *tells* the man and the woman, but *why he made them in the first place.*

Not only the *order* in which God created human beings, but the *way* he went about making them is significant. In the first five days of Creation God had said, "Let there be . . . and it was so." We are simply told what God did. But the sixth day is different. For the first time we are told not only *what* God did, but *why* he did it. We are told first of God *planning* the creation of humankind (v. 26) and only then of his actually carrying out the plan (v. 27). The plan is deliberately to make humankind "to be our image and to rule" over the earth. Thus "ruling" is a fundamental part of God's *creative act itself;* it is *built into* the very way that God planned not only human beings but even the rest of the world.

God made human beings precisely in order to care for the earth. We were made to serve this purpose. It is built into our very being; it is our very design. We are purpose-built creatures. If we do not take up our responsibility for God's world, we defy not only his command, but also our very nature and the very purpose for which we have been created. Our responsibility for the world is a fundamental part of God's plan of creation.

IN THE IMAGE OF THE CREATOR

The same theme is expressed when we are taught that we are made "in the image" of God. To be in the image of God is to be like him in some way. The Bible describes several different expressions of this image—the New Testament mentions righteousness, holiness, and knowledge as reflections of our imaging. In Genesis the image—one of the ways in which we are like God—seems to refer specifically to our being God's representatives on the earth and to our having dominion over, and responsibility for, creation.

Genesis 1:26 reads, "Let us make man in our image, after our likeness; and let them rule. . . ." It is more accurately translated, "Let us make man in our image . . . *in order that* they might rule." This is the same theme as found in the Psalms: "Thou has given him dominion over the works of thy hands, thou hast put all things under his feet" (Ps. 8:5–6, KJV). Our dominion over the earth is one way in which we are like God. When we follow God's purpose in making the world and in making us in the world as stewards of all creation, then we are manifesting part of the image of God. We are called to image God by our activities in ruling, forming, and caring for God's creation.

We'll return to this theme many times. It is essential in understanding our purpose and how God calls us to live. It appears first right at the beginning of the Bible, and the Bible never abandons or rejects it. As we will see, even sin does not destroy our human responsibility. Our redemption in Jesus Christ does not remove that responsibility; it restores and renews our calling as part of the drama of salvation.

WHAT IS THE "WORLD"?

Perhaps we are reluctant to recognize our place in God's world or to treat the world as good because we recall that the Bible tells us *not* to love the world. Indeed we know all too well the frequent scriptural denunciations of the "world." Paul says, "[Let] those who use the things of the world, [use them] as if not engrossed in them. For this world in its present form is passing away" (1 Cor. 7:31).

In Romans he says, "Do not conform any longer to the pattern of this world. . . . " (12:2)

Speaking to Pontius Pilate, Jesus said, "My kingdom is not of this world" (John 18:36).

James tells us to keep ourselves "from being polluted by the world" (James 1:27).

In the Gospel of John, we are told that we "do not belong to the world, but I have chosen you out of the world. That is why the world hates you." (John 15:19).

These examples could be multiplied, yet they do not contradict the teaching about the goodness of the world.[1]

World has several meanings in the Bible. One meaning refers to the sinful aspects of the world, particularly to the way humans have wrongfully ordered the world, especially society. This is the meaning in the verses we have just quoted. A more accurate rendition of Romans 12:2 would be "don't be conformed to this age," or "don't do what everybody else does," or "don't let the non-Christian world set your standards for you." We should follow the ways of the Lord, not the ways of the godless culture in which we live.

Another meaning refers to geography or territory, as in "this gospel will be preached throughout the whole world" (Matt. 24:14).

A third meaning of world is "the created order," that which God has made, and made for us to live in. That is what the word meant in Genesis: the world that God loves and to which he will be reconciled. For Jesus came "not to condemn the world, but that the world might be saved through him" (John 3:17). That is why there is no contradiction between John's saying, "Do not love the world...." (1 John 2:15) and "For God so loved the world that he gave his only begotten Son...." (John 3:16).

God rejects the sinful world that fallen humanity tries to create. But he loves the world he has made. So should we.

SWIMMING WITH THE SHARKS

Yehuda loves sharks. Most days out in the boat he would begin by lecturing about them and showing videos of them. Later, if we were lucky, the sharks themselves would appear, drawn by a line of blood and fractured fish that streamed behind us. Then we'd get into the cage and gaze at them as they swam relentlessly and (seemingly) menacingly about us, looking for the source of the food they had smelled from miles away.

Divers are allowed out of the cage in pairs to go and swim with the sharks. We were not sent out entirely unarmed, however. Each of us was given an eighteen-inch piece of light plastic tubing for protection. Such weak armament was not very reassuring, but all we'd have to do, if a shark came too close, was to push it gently away with the stick. Sharks have skin like sandpaper, and if you try to push them by hand, you might find yourself suffering from a shortage of skin.

If the art of pushing didn't seem to work, then we were to bop the shark on the nose with the tube. Since their noses are very sensitive, this usually drives them away. We were cautioned that if at all possible, we should avoid bopping them on the nose. This had nothing to do with our safety but simply with the fact that Yehuda didn't want the sharks scared off before the other divers had a chance to swim with them, too.

As my diving partner and I (the first pair of the day) prepared to dive into the waters off Catalina, we saw two blue sharks circling. The enthusiastic crew and passengers gathered at the rear ladder to encourage us with jeers and catcalls. The last thing we heard before our feet touched the water was the crew chanting the theme from Jaws. However, the sharks were as well behaved as promised. They required no pushing or bopping: mainly they seemed interested in having us get out of the way so they could find the real food.

After we were all back in the boat embellishing our stories for one another, we received more shark lessons as we described their behavior. Then it was time for "shark tagging." This meant putting identification markers on sharks so that if they were found again, we could trace something of their life history. Not much is known about sharks. We don't really know how long they live, nor how far they travel. Do they hang around in the same area, or do they traverse the ocean endlessly?

Another thing about sharks that worried Yehuda is that there are signs that the creatures are becoming endangered. But it's very hard to arouse public sympathy over this, even though people will rally to protect other endangered species. Giant pandas look cuddly and nice. Condors are soaring and majestic. Tigers are beautiful and, though dangerous, live far away from us.

But tell people that sharks are endangered, and all you're likely to get is a rousing cheer followed by enthusiastic applause. People are more worried about coming back out of the ocean with all their body parts still intact than they are about the fate of creatures they fear might have them for lunch.

Yehuda works continuously to get people interested in sharks and their well-being. My most endearing memory of him came as we toured the tanks at the Marine Center. In mid-discourse, Yehuda reached into a tank and pulled out one of his favorite sharks to use as a visual aid. Then, smiling happily, Yehuda gave the little guy a big kiss, right on its sensitive nose, before returning it to its tank.

STEWARDS OF NATURE, AND OF MUCH MORE

We have all been called to be stewards of creation. This means something different for each of us. Most of us envision ourselves tending gardens—flowers, herbs, trees, or backyard lawns—as the first couple was instructed to do. We contemplate the beauties of mountains, deserts, seas, and plains. We reflect upon modern environmental concerns and wonder how far stewardship should extend. To protecting endangered species? Eliminating pollution? Simple recycling? There are myriad other ecological issues, many of them requiring some action on our part, for the natural world is a vital part of our responsibility.

But caring for the creation extends far beyond the boundaries of earth, oceans, sky, and clouds. We human beings, we *ourselves*, are part of creation. Our stewardship includes human life as well as the rest of nature. It includes Mozart as well as mountains; parliaments as well as porpoises; friendships as well as fields and forests. What began in the Garden of Eden culminates in a city— the New Jerusalem. Creation includes culture as well as nature. And although the entire creation has been corrupted by sin, it still remains the realm over which we have been given responsibility.

Caring for creation—stars, cars, scars, and all—is the reason we were made.

three

OUR STRUGGLE WITH SIN

As South Africa's evil system of apartheid was being abolished and the country prepared for its first genuinely nonracial election, I talked in the town of Potchefstroom with a group of earnest young Afrikaner students. They had not built apartheid, but they had grown up under it and had benefited from it. They still held positions of privilege that the system had produced. Now, under the critical eye of the world, they faced an uncertain future.

These young Christians needed to come to terms with their history, especially as it touched their own families. How could their parents, who had always been so loving and kind and deeply spiritual, have held other races in their grip? Their parents had cared tenderly for their children all their lives. But, to maintain their control, most of them had also participated, or at least stood quietly by, as blood was shed in the streets.

Both sides of their parents were real. How did they fit together?

As we talked, it became clear that one root of the sin had been exceedingly subtle. Certainly there was greed, hatred, and lust for *power. But the Afrikaners had always claimed to be a deeply Christian people, living and growing in a strange and threatening land. They were as sure of, were as possessed by, a sense of divine calling as was ancient Israel or the New England Puritans. They thought their first responsibility to God was to preserve themselves as a Christian people.*

At first, this motive seemed to be a good one, even a holy one. Even now, it seems like a simple misplacement of loyalty. But the misplacement ran deep; ultimately, their chief mission before God was no longer to do God's will but their own preservation as God's people. In the end, no barrier, no rule, no higher priority, not even another people could be allowed to stand in the way, for they must be preserved. From this root sprang the grievous injustice that followed. The end result was racism, persecution, bloodshed, and death.

The Afrikaners are a good example of how even good people can make choices that are an affront to God. "Satan himself masquerades as an angel of light. It is not surprising then, if his servants masquerade as servants of righteousness" (2 Cor. 11:14). Sin usually does not first appear ominous or foreboding. It usually appears as a good thing, only slightly twisted. But it leads to death.

Early, very early, in the life of the human race, we perverted God's plan. Instead of walking with God and caring for the world, Adam and Eve disobeyed. They wanted not only to be *like* God (which they were); they wanted to *be* God, and so they ate the fruit of the tree that had been forbidden to them. Once they had broken with God's will, humanity, and consequently the whole world, became marked by evil, by corruption, and by pain.

BROKEN RELATIONSHIPS

When they ate of the fruit of the tree, the man and the woman became separated from God, and they hid from him (Gen. 3:8). Our relation to God is always at the core of sin. Eve and Adam had been called to live in God's presence and to rejoice in him. But their disobedience had severed the relationship that had anchored their life. As the inevitable consequence, every other relation within the world was also severed and corrupted. Through their sin, they were cut off from their Creator, from themselves, from each other, from the natural world, and from the generations to follow.

After they had sinned, Adam and Eve were ashamed of their nakedness and tried to cover themselves. Their previous unselfconscious openness was replaced by fear and a struggle to hide from God, from each other, and even from facing themselves (v. 7). They could no longer face who they were, and so they covered themselves. We have remained in hiding from God and from one another ever since.

Adam and Eve also immediately turned against each other. When God asked Adam why he ate the fruit, he replied, "The woman who you put with me . . . gave [it] to me," implicitly blaming first Eve, then God himself, for the whole thing (v. 12, NJB). When God then asked Eve why she did it, she in turn blamed the serpent (v. 13). Everybody blamed somebody else. We have blamed each other, and blamed God, ever since.

As a result of their sin, Adam and Eve's relationship was corrupted on a personal level, but on a much broader scale as well. Their relation as two different *types* of people, as man and woman, was also betrayed. Whereas before, humankind had been given an authority over the animals, an authority that was manifested in Adam's power to name them (2:19, 20), now the man went beyond this and tried to rule over the woman in the way that he had been asked to rule over the animals (v. 23). Man and woman were driven apart and have remained apart ever since.

SIN'S FAR-REACHING EFFECTS

Because God has given humankind such great authority and responsibility in the world, the consequences of our sin affect the whole creation. Sin makes even the earth become corrupted: "Cursed is the ground because of you; through painful toil you will eat of it all the days of your life. It will produce thorns and thistles for you. . . . " (Gen. 3:17–18).

The curse that God pronounced here is *not* that Adam henceforth would have to work. Human work *already existed* before the Fall—it was one of the reasons we were created. The man was already settled "in the Garden of Eden to work it and take care of it" (2:15). Sin is not the reason we have to work, but it is what makes our work miserable "painful toil." Adam would henceforth eat by "the sweat of his brow" (vv. 17–19), struggling with weeds and thorns.

Even childbirth was corrupted by sin. Eve was told that "with pain you will give birth to children" (3:16). This curse referred not to the actual pain of labor in childbirth, but to the children themselves, the ones who will result from that labor.

A few verses later we read that Eve conceived and bore Cain (4:1). And then she bore Abel. *Cain killed Abel.* Cain was the first murderer, and Abel was the first murder victim. Of Eve's two children, the first births recorded in the Bible, one was murdered and the other was a murderer. Few greater agonies could befall a parent. While the pangs of labor still contain the seed of hope, the destruction of children, physically and morally, brings despair.

As a result of the curse, bringing children into the world would no longer be a source of unalloyed joy and hope, the unmitigated expectation of future intimacy, pleasure, and achievement. It would always be tinged with apprehension and fear for, with sin loose in the world, who knows what grief might loom ahead?

SIN'S VICIOUS CIRCLE

It was not only Adam and Eve's relation with their own children that was affected by their sin. The effect of the curse would touch their children, and their children's children, right on throughout human history. Sin and its effects would tarnish and corrupt every subsequent human act and thought and desire, including our divine task of caring for the world. Human history became derailed, and it has remained so ever since.

In his great theological analysis in his letter to the Romans, Paul provides a commentary on Genesis and describes this rapid spread of the consequences of sin as "death spread to all men" (Rom. 5:12). He speaks of the "reign of death" (Rom. 5:21) in which "the creation was subjected to futility" and "bondage to decay" so that "the whole creation has been groaning in travail" (Rom. 8:20–22). Sin and death have touched everything. Nothing is immune. No human being, no husband or wife or child, no thought or word or act, no hope or dream is free from the effect of that awful calamity.

This fast-spreading circle of sin's effects shows the powerful effects of human rule and responsibility. If the ruler of a country is corrupt, then that country will feel the effects right down to the last inhabitant. If the boss of a company is corrupt, then that company will feel the effects right down to the last employee or customer. If a parent is corrupt, then the children and the children's children will bear the effects. Those in authority spread their sin, and the consequences of their sin, to others. And since, under God, human beings have been given authority for the entire creation, then the entire creation suffers to the ends of the earth.

LIFEBOAT THEOLOGY

Perhaps, at this point, our reaction might be, "Why are you talking about this ancient history? Hasn't sin ended the good creation? God's original intention, for us to be the stewards of the earth, no longer applies to us because of sin. We've wrecked the world: what's important now is simply that we rescue people from the wreckage."

This point of view might be called "lifeboat theology." It is as if the creation were the *Titanic,* and now that we've hit the iceberg of sin, there's nothing left for us to do but get ourselves into lifeboats. The ship is sinking rapidly, God has given up on it and is concerned only with the survival of his people. Any effort we make to salvage God's creation amounts to rearranging the deck chairs. Instead, some say, our sole task is to get into the lifeboats, to keep them afloat, to pluck drowning victims out of the water, and to sail on until we get to heaven where all will be well.

However, a truly Christian viewpoint is not "lifeboat theology," but "ark theology" instead. Noah's ark saved not only *people,* but it preserved God's other creatures as well. The ark looked not to flee but to return to the land and begin again. Once the flood subsided, *everyone and everything aboard was intended to return again to restore the earth.* In Noah's day, God sent the flood in response to humankind's fall into sin. But the story of the generations of Noah shows that *even after the fall God still has the same purpose in mind for human beings.* Humankind was given a fresh start and new help and was set about its life task once more. God established a covenant that never again would the earth be destroyed by flood and pointed to the rainbow as the sign of the covenant.

This covenant, one of the dominant themes of the Bible, was made not only with Noah and his descendants, but with the animals also: "with every living creature that is with you, the birds, the cattle, and every beast of the earth with you, as many as came out of the ark" (Gen. 9:10). The rainbow was still an eternal sign between God "and every living creature of all flesh" (9:12, 15, 16, 17). God cares for and keeps faith *with all of the creation.* God is still committed to the preservation of the world and to the ongoing process of human history.

The story of Noah demonstrates that God has not given up on the world. God said to Noah, *after the fall,* what he had said to Adam and Eve, *before the fall:* "multiply and replenish." With Noah, the cycle of human life began once more, and immediately we read that Noah, "a man of the soil, proceeded to plant a vineyard" (9:20), and that from his children "came the people who were scattered over the earth" (9:19).

From these children "peoples spread out into their territories by their clans within their nations, each with its own language" (10:5). From them came Nimrod "who grew to be a mighty warrior on the earth. He was a mighty hunter before the LORD" (10:8, 9). The spread and activity of the human population, for a time, seemed to indicate that perhaps people would take up their God-given responsibilities in obedient and healing ways. But humankind went astray yet again and diverted their energies into an effort to become gods by constructing Babel, a tower that would reach to the heavens. And so the Lord intervened and scattered them abroad (11:1–9). God's hand remains on all of the creation. He wants and wills to save them.

What was true then remains true now: God *still* cares for the creation and for human life, and humanity still disobeys him.

Sin is not the story; it is the blight on the story. Sin distorts everything, perverts everything, corrupts everything. It is not sin that makes us bear children, but it is sin that makes childbearing painful. It is not sin that attracts men and women, but it is sin that fills our relations with control and suspicion. It is not sin that makes music, but it is sin that fills our songs with vanity and lust. It is not sin that makes us construct cities and towers, but it is sin that makes those towers symbols of pride and power. It is not sin that calls human beings to live and love, to make music and art, to work and create, to plant and harvest, to play and dance. But it is sin that undercuts and perverts them all.

Sin does not create things. It has no originality, no creativity, no being in itself. Sin lives off that which is good. It is a parasite, feeding greedily on the goodness of what God has made. No relation is of itself sinful, but sin corrupts every relation. No area of life is in itself out of the will of God, but we defy God's will in every area of life.

It is not sin that gives us freedom of choice. But it is sin that makes us take the wrong path. Hence, what we need is *not* to be rescued from the world, not to cease being human, not to stop caring for the world, not to stop shaping human culture. *What we need is the power to do these things according to the will of God.* We, as well as the rest of creation, need to be redeemed. It is to that redemption we now turn.

four

R EDEMPTION
AND HUMAN LIFE

Walking down the street in a small village in central Java, I was carrying a parrot and feeling very uncomfortable about it. It wasn't the parrot's fault. Fred was a cute little guy and quite friendly. He made occasional clucking noises and preened his wings, even though he was a bit nervous about all the new and strange sights and sounds.

But there was a problem: what was I going to do with a parrot? I couldn't take him back to Canada. They wouldn't allow a parrot on the plane, and I assumed that a live bird couldn't be shipped. And how was I supposed to carry him (I think it was a "him," but wasn't sure) around Indonesia for the next three weeks?

I had ended up with the parrot because I had momentarily forgotten a rule that one needs to remember when dealing with people in many other countries, especially so-called third world countries. Many of these people, not having much, not expecting much, and not having been reared with western caution, are quite free in giving things to guests. It's a powerful and beautiful impulse. But it means that, as a guest, you must be careful not to admire an ornament, a curtain, or a piece of cloth or furniture too much. Otherwise, it may be given to you. You must be especially careful not to admire a parrot. Much less a water buffalo.

It does no good to protest that you are wealthy and your hosts are poor. Nor would it be helpful to explain that you do not need it. All of these concerns are quite beside the point. The point is that it is a gift. It is not earned. It is not calculated. It is not deserved. It is a free act of love and generosity. It is a picture of how God deals with us.

God's love and generosity are interwoven throughout the earliest biblical stories—in his clothing Adam and Eve (Gen. 3:21), in his mercy toward Cain (Gen. 4:15), in the rescue of Noah and his family from the flood (Gen. 6–7). None of these things were deserved. Nobody had a right to such gifts; sin had forfeited any such right. But God gave and cared and loved anyway. He never gave up loving, and his hand remained on human life and on the creation itself.

GOD'S HAND OF REDEMPTION THROUGH ABRAHAM

After the story of human lust for power in the construction of the tower of Babel (Gen. 11:1–8), Genesis moves on more rapidly and lists the succeeding generations of people without much comment until we come to the account of the generations of Terah (11:27). Terah lived in Ur of the Chaldees, but later took his family on to Haran. And it is in Haran that God once again set out to bring humankind lovingly back to the truth and to redirect their paths into his will. God appears to one of Terah's children, the one we now call Abraham, and says to him,

> *Leave your country, your people and your father's household and*
> *go to the land I will show you. I will make you into a great nation*
> *and I will bless you; I will make your name great, and you will be*
> *a blessing. I will bless those who bless you, and whoever curses you*
> *I will curse; and all peoples on earth will be blessed through you.*
>
> Genesis 12:1–3

Abraham is introduced as one whose divine destiny is to bring God's blessing to "all the families of the earth." Paul describes this promise as God saying to Abraham that "he would be heir of the world" (Rom. 4:13). God's concern for Abraham reflects his concern for the whole world.

And so God's plan of redemption begins to be revealed. Through Abram and Sarah, one would come to forgive human sins, set us right with God, and lead all creatures, indeed, all the world, back into paths of peaceful, loving service. As Paul says: "Therefore, just as sin entered the world through one man, and death through sin, and in this way death came to all men, because all sinned . . . how much more did God's grace and the gift that came by the grace of the one man, Jesus Christ, overflow to the many!" (Rom. 5:12, 15).

Notice how, throughout the book of Genesis the focus of the salvation story continues to narrow. From the drama of the heavens and earth we move closer in order to see the history of humankind. From the history of humankind we move closer to see the history of the children of Shem, the Semites. From the history of the Semites we move closer to see the history of Abraham and Sarah.

With the introduction of the children of Abraham and Sarah, the Scriptures now focus on the drama of God's redemptive plan, first through Israel and ultimately through Jesus Christ, the Messiah that Israel will bring forth.

Up to this point, the Bible has shown us how we were made, what we were made for, and why we are here. It has shown us what went wrong and how evil has spread throughout God's good world. *Now it shows us God's solution, the key to our salvation, healing, restoration, and renewal, and therefore to the healing, restoration, and renewal of the world.*

The Bible is the story of how sin has been, is being, and will be overcome through Jesus Christ. It is the story of how humankind has been, is being, and will be redeemed and restored to fellowship with God. The creatures God has made to love and rule and steward the earth will be redeemed. Redemption means *to bring back, to buy back, to restore.* The Bible is given to us to reveal this message.

GOD'S UNBROKEN PROMISE TO A NATION IN EXILE

The history of Israel is the history of the people God has chosen and with whom God has covenanted. God's concern with the people of Israel is not only with their "spiritual" life—how they sacrifice and pray—but also with *every part of their life.* After saving them from slavery in Egypt, he teaches them in the Law how they are to conduct themselves in every facet of life: how to divide up the land, how to make decisions about marriage, how to bring up children, and how to handle and punish murder and theft.

God is concerned with *all* of Israel's life. And not only theirs: he is concerned with *all of the world.* Hence, gradually it becomes clear to Israel that God wants *all* the nations to live in the way that

Israel is called to live. Israel was chosen not only for its own sake, but also to be a model, an example, a sign to all the nations. This becomes clear in the book of Daniel.

In the book of Daniel, Israel is a nation in exile. The Israelites had been defeated in battle, and the nation's leaders taken prisoner into Babylon. Daniel and his friends were torn from the Promised Land and transported to the center of what was then the world's greatest empire. In terms of ancient world politics, Daniel came from a forgotten backwater country. Israel was small, with hardly enough resources to make it worth the time for a mighty empire to invade it. Israel's major claim to world attention was that it stood across the major routes connecting the centers of world powers. As far as the major military and commercial forces were concerned, Israel was an awkward place, merely in the way.

Except for a relatively small expansion it had enjoyed under David and Solomon, Israel was primarily a buffer state in the wars and competing claims among the empires of Egypt, Assyria, and Babylon. But out of this obscure place, remarkable only for the fact that its people seemed to be obsessed with the claim that their God was the God-over-all-gods, Daniel rose to become an adviser to the world's greatest empire.

Since Daniel wanted to remain faithful to the Lord, he struggled earnestly to discover how God wanted him to advise this empire. What do you do as a believer in a strange and ungodly land? What was God's calling to non-Israelites? In the book of Daniel we see the redemptive purposes of God now being played out, not just in Israel but also in the relations between the most powerful nations of the then-known world.

After God spoke to Daniel concerning King Nebuchadnezzar's dream, Daniel exclaimed, "He changes times and seasons; he sets up kings and deposes them" (Dan. 2:21). He learned that God rules over not only Israel, but over Babylon too.

Even Nebuchadnezzar himself had to acknowledge, "Surely your God is the God of gods and the Lord of kings. . . . " (2:47). Israel's God was not a local god: he claimed Babylon (and Assyria and Persia and Egypt and Rome) as well.

This theme is repeated throughout the book of Daniel: "His kingdom is an eternal kingdom; his dominion endures from generation to generation" (4:3). At the end of his life, even Nebuchadnezzar realizes the same thing: "His dominion is an eternal dominion; his kingdom endures from generation to generation" (4:34). Later Daniel points out to King Belshazzar,

> *The Most High God gave your father Nebuchadnezzar sovereignty and greatness and glory and splendor. . . . But when his heart became arrogant and hardened with pride, he was deposed from his royal throne and stripped of his glory . . . until he acknowledged that the Most High God is sovereign over the kingdoms of men. . . . But you his son, O Belshazzar . . . you did not honor the God who holds in his hand your life and all your ways.*
>
> Daniel 5:18–23

Daniel said that Nebuchadnezzar had kingship only because God gave it to him and that he was deposed until he acknowledged the one true God from whom his authority came. Therefore Belshazzar, his royal son, must do the same. Babylon, too, belonged to God, and its rulers were his servants. Later even

Darius the Great had to decree, "For he is the living God and he endures forever; his kingdom will not be destroyed, his dominion will never end" (6:26). God is the God not only of Abraham and David, but also of Belshazzar and Darius.

This is the continual theme of Daniel—that God is the God not only of Israel, but also of the whole earth. God's dominion still goes on throughout history—from people to people, from generation to generation. It does not stop after the generations listed in Genesis: God's dominion covers all kingdoms, all empires. Ultimately, even these kingdoms are subject to God's law and will pass into God's own kingdom of love and righteousness.

As the people of Israel begin to spill over onto the world stage, so it starts to become clear that the God of the whole world is also the Redeemer of the whole world. What God plans to do he will do not only for Israel, but also for Babylon, for Rome, and for whatever empire follows. Daniel tells us that God's purpose in choosing Israel takes in the whole world, that God's dominion continues and will not cease. Jesus himself picks up this theme in the Great Commission when he tells his disciples: "Make disciples of all nations teaching them to obey everything I have commanded you" (Matt. 28:19–20).

GOD'S NEW TESTAMENT COVENANT

This focus on the entire world is not limited to the Old Testament or to Old Covenant policies that passed away when Jesus came. They permeate the New Testament as well. God's New Covenant in Jesus Christ is a covenant that continues to embrace the whole earth. John's Gospel deliberately parallels the opening words of Genesis when it says, "In the beginning was the Word. . . . " (John 1:1).

Jesus does not come into the story merely halfway through. He is the one who was already there *at the beginning.* He is the one *through whom the world was made.* He is the source of life. Jesus is the Creator as well as the Redeemer. In fact, he is the Redeemer of the world because he is its Creator.

Paul reiterates this theme in Romans. After showing the significance of Abraham for the redemption not only of Israel but also of the world (chapter 4), and after proclaiming that all of what one man, Adam, corrupted will be restored in one man, Jesus Christ (chapter 5), Paul describes the effect of sin and the place of the law and of faith (chapters 6 and 7).

In chapter 8 Paul rejoices that "the law of the Spirit of life set me free from the law of sin and death" (8:1), and he shows how the just requirements of the law might now be fulfilled (8:4). Because of this we have now become children of God, who cry "Abba! Father!" and are heirs of God (8:15–17).

Paul does not stop there. This is neither the end of his story, nor the end of the Gospel. He rushes breathlessly on to show an even wider significance of our restoration as children of God— *that it is a promise in Jesus Christ not just to us, but also to the creation itself.*

> *The creation waits in eager expectation for the sons of God to be revealed. For the creation was subjected to frustration, not by its own choice, but by the will of the one who subjected it, in hope that the creation itself will be liberated from its bondage to decay and brought into the glorious freedom of the children of God. We know*

that the whole creation has been groaning as in the pains of child-
birth right up to the present time. Not only so, but we ourselves,
who have the firstfruits of the Spirit, groan inwardly as we wait
eagerly for our adoption as sons, the redemption of our bodies.

Romans 8:19–23

In this glorious climax announcing the liberty in the Spirit of the children of God, Paul says that even this amazing announcement is not all. Not only do *we* suffer, but *the creation itself* also suffers because of the effects of sin. Not only *we* wait eagerly, but *the creation itself* also waits eagerly for freedom from oppression. Not only *we* will be set free, but *the creation itself* will also be set free just as (and because) the children of God are set free. Paul exults that God's redemption is for the creation—*everything* that God has made. The redemption of humankind in Jesus Christ also means, through the renewing of our task to care for the world, the restoration of the world itself. This is one reason why "neither death nor life, neither angels nor demons, neither the present nor the future, nor any powers, neither height nor depth, nor anything else in all creation, will be able to separate us from the love of God that is in Christ Jesus our Lord" (8:39).

Paul does not mean that each and every individual thing, or each and every individual person, will be saved, for he directly goes on to talk about God's election, God's choice of some. His point is not that every individual person or every individual thing will be rescued, but that *all sorts of things* will be rescued. Just as Adam's sin has affected everything, so also will redemption in Christ affect everything. Redemption in Jesus Christ is not limited to any one area of the creation: souls, persons, nations, kingdoms, mountains, rivers, seas—the entire creation will be reconciled. God, through Jesus Christ, will make a new heaven and a new earth wherein righteousness dwells. God will make *all things new* (Rev. 21:5).

After his discussion of Israel and the Church, Paul sums up by proclaiming: "for from him and through him and to him are all things" (Rom. 11:36). Then he tells the Church at Rome what this redemption means for how they must now live.

He tells them to "offer your bodies as living sacrifices" and that this living sacrificial life is itself an "act of spiritual worship" (12:1).

They must not be conformed to the patterns of this present age (or present world) but, by living as God has commanded, be the transformed forerunners and firstfruits of the new age (12:2).

He tells them to judge their abilities and gifts soberly (12:3), for they each have different gifts; each will do a different type of thing in the restoration of creation (12:6–8).

He tells them that they are not just individuals but that they are "individually members one of another." The new people in Christ are members of a body fitted together, who have a communal task in the world (12:4–5).

Paul goes on to give advice for those with different kinds of gifts—prophets, administrators, teachers, preachers, almsgivers, officials, and doers of works of mercy (12:6, 7).

He tells them how to do these tasks, hating evil, loving good, with zeal, patience, constancy in prayer, generosity, tears, rejoicing, harmony, humility, forgiveness, and peacefulness (12:9–20).

He sums up our Christian task in the world with the words "do not be overcome with evil, but overcome evil with good"

(12:21)—withstand and reverse the effects of sin, overcome evil so that love and righteousness and peace may prevail in the world.

Having given these general instructions for God's new people in all their service in God's world, Paul turns his attention to particular examples and areas of service. He tells them what to do in relation to government (13:1–7), debts (13:8), the law (13:8–10), eating taboos (14:1–4), special days (14:5–9), and judgments (14:10–13). He points out that "nothing is unclean in itself" (14:14), that is, nothing in creation is, in and of itself, a forbidden thing for Christians to use. Every dimension of life is to be lived in Jesus Christ and to be transformed by a renewing of our minds and hearts.

These are not isolated or incidental texts and themes. They are at the core of the letter to the Romans, the most systematic theological writing in the New Testament. When Paul gives a systematic overview of the gospel in any of his letters, he invariably expounds Jesus' cosmic significance—that Jesus is the Savior of the world.[1]

Perhaps the best of many examples is in the first chapter of his letter to the Colossians, where Paul drives home the message that the gospel shapes *all things*. In what is probably an early Christian hymn or prayer, he says of Jesus:

> *He is the image of the invisible God, the firstborn over all creation. For by him all things were created: things in heaven and on earth, visible and invisible, whether thrones or powers or rulers or authorities; all things were created by him and for him. He is before all things, and in him all things hold together. And he is the head of the body, the church; he is the beginning and the firstborn from among the dead, so that in everything he might have the*

supremacy. For God was pleased to have all his fullness dwell in him, and through him to reconcile to himself all things, whether things on earth or things in heaven, by making peace through his blood, shed on the cross.

Colossians 1:15–20

Here Paul stresses that the gospel is *for all things,* and he makes a threefold statement about the lordship of Christ. *Everything was made by and for Jesus Christ. Everything holds together in Jesus Christ. Everything will be reconciled by Jesus Christ.* The "everything" that is reconciled is the same everything that was made. The scope of redemption is the same as the scope of creation. The Creator and Redeemer are one and the same. Things in heaven, things in earth, things visible and invisible, dominions, and authorities will be reconciled by the cross of Jesus Christ (see also Heb. 1:1–3).

Paul says that redemption is cosmic in scope, that God will restore what has been lost through sin. Through Jesus Christ, humankind will take its rightful place in the creation and mold the world in love and obedience to God. God will reconcile "all things" to himself through Jesus Christ. Was there ever a greater promise stated or thought or dreamed? Who can conceive so great a salvation?

This deep understanding that each facet of existence, everything that God has made, is caught up in the redemption of Jesus Christ permeates the understanding of salvation in the Old and New Testament alike. God loves the world, and one of the ways in which this is evident is in his grace, compassion, and discipline in the arena of human culture and achievement.

Human life in the world is not ended or dismissed by redemption in Jesus Christ. It is renewed and put back on track. What we do in our everyday lives—in or out of church—is part of God's purpose for our lives. We need to live each and every day a life that demonstrates the redeeming power of God in our prayer, our programming, our play, and our politics. This is a joyful calling, though not an easy one. In the rest of this book, we will consider how we can and should respond to God's gift of grace in all of life.

> *About Fred, the parrot: I had learned a little, so I waited until someone else admired him. Then I quickly and generously (and perhaps selfishly) gave Fred away. Maybe Fred moved on again, never bought, never earned, but freely given. He didn't know that he had become a symbol of grace. And that's how it should be.*

OUR RESPONSE

TO THE WORLD

PART III

five

THE WONDER OF LEARNING

The island of Culion lies in a remote area of the southwestern Philippines. Its main community is centered around a leprosy hospital. I was scared about the idea of going into a "leper colony"—scared about how I would react upon meeting people who lacked fingers, or hands, or eyes, or noses. Scared that I would show revulsion and so insult someone. Scared that I would cringe if, shaking hands with somebody, I would find that person's "hand" was something else. But once I was actually at Culion, this feeling soon passed away. When you meet people as people and learn their joys, pains, griefs, fears, and hopes, pretty soon you don't much notice what they look like.

On a second trip we were asked to visit the wards to lead worship services. The wards contained the hardest-hit patients, those who could no longer walk and were almost helpless. Once again, in my usual self-absorbed way, I was worried. I assumed that, since I speak to a lot of groups, I would be asked to speak, and what on earth could I possibly say to them that would be insightful or useful? Of what use is a western professor in a remote Asian leprosy ward?

As it turned out, nobody was remotely interested in hearing me speak. Instead, they requested something that was even more daunting—that we sing for them. I had never sung publicly in my life and had no desire to (nor does anyone who's ever heard me sing ask for a repeat performance). But there, standing in a ramshackle ward among forgotten people on an island in the Sulu Sea, I was suddenly given a choice. I could turn down the only request that those people had made of me. Or I could stop thinking about myself for once, put myself in God's hands, and get up and sing.

We sang. And they enjoyed it, or at least they had the kindness to say they did.

I have learned many things and have several academic degrees framed on the wall. I suppose they are important for some things, but they mean much less to me now than they did when I first earned them. They symbolize the mastery of a body of information or the acquisition of a skill. We need these, for we live in a complex world. But they don't symbolize the heart of learning.

Real learning occurs when we face something new. It is a struggle for which we are unprepared, a challenge to the rhythm of our thoughts and actions. The heart of learning appears when we learn how to change, to grow, to adjust, to become something different. Universities can help, but it's the leper colonies, the demands of humility or courage, that teach us best.

THE WORLD IS GOD'S SCHOOLMASTER

We have no choice but to learn. Babies, students, parents, and teachers—everyone must learn. We need to grow intellectually, as well as physically, morally, and spiritually. God has made us creatures who must change, adapt, adjust, and develop. Our life and our skills are not given to us finished all at once. Throughout the course of our lives, we have to discover and mature.

The gifts we have learned to use most efficiently are not always the gifts that people want from us. And the gifts that God requires us to use may be things we have to learn and re-learn in every new situation. Learning, in the Christian life, is not merely a process of acquiring more information or even a more solid grounding from the Bible. Nor is it simply being better informed or developing new skills. The most basic form of learning happens in situations—like my trip to Culion—when we face something very new and have to find a new way to respond. For this reason, our calling as Christians is not only to know the Bible, though we certainly need to know it verse by verse. It is also to *know the world* where God has placed us and to learn from that world.

God's purposes and our calling in the world are always ongoing: New questions, new problems, new challenges, new hopes will arise. We are called to grow, to question and to deepen in knowledge and wisdom. This requires change—not just any change, but change in line with the will of God. In the Bible, God has revealed to us the fundamental realities of human existence and shown us the direction in which we should go. But the Bible itself does not, nor is intended to, teach us *everything* we should know. *In fact it teaches us that it does not teach us everything we need to know.* Rather, in its light, we are to investigate and understand the world itself. This learning is an endless adventure, an adventure whose directions and ends we often cannot imagine.

Wherever and whatever we genuinely learn in the world, we usually learn from many people and many things. But it is always God who is our ultimate teacher. Isaiah asks,

> *When a farmer plows for planting, does he plow continually?*
> *Does he keep on breaking up and harrowing the soil?*
> *When he has leveled the surface,*
> *does he not sow caraway and scatter cummin?*
> *Does he not plant wheat in its place,*
> *barley in its plot,*
> *and spelt in its field?*
> *His God instructs him*
> *and teaches him the right way.*
>
> *Caraway is not threshed with a sledge,*
> *nor is a cartwheel rolled over cummin;*
> *Caraway is beaten out with a rod,*
> *and cummin with a stick.*
> *Grain must be ground to make bread;*
> *so one does not go on threshing it forever.*
> *Though he drives the wheels of his threshing cart over*
> *it, his horses do not grind it.*
> *All this also comes from the Lord Almighty*
> *wonderful in counsel and magnificent in wisdom.*

Isaiah 28:23–29

Isaiah does not mean that the farmer simply sits down and prays until God finally says, "This is how you use a plow" or "This is how you grind grain." The farmer likely learned it from his father and mother, who did it before him. He learned it from his neighbors, who could advise him on what they did. He learned it from experience: you don't just keep turning the soil—it's a waste of time. Instead you turn it just enough for the seed to find its place in the earth. You don't keep on grinding grain, or you'll just end up with powder. You do it until the grain is fine enough to make bread.

This kind of learning comes from teaching, advice, experience, and from paying careful attention to what the world brings us. But this is not opposed to learning from God's Word. It is not an either/or choice of whether we learn from God or from experience. Isaiah says that whenever we properly learn from experience, it is in fact God who is the teacher. The world itself is God's schoolmaster. As Martin Luther said,

> *If you are a manual laborer, you find that the Bible has been put into your workshop, into your hand, into your heart. It teaches and preaches how you should treat you neighbour. . . . Just look at your tools . . . at your needle and thimble, your beer barrel, your goods, your scales or yardstick or measure. . . . You have as many preachers as you have transactions, goods, tools, and other equipment in your house and home.[1]*

God is the farmer's teacher, and he is ours as well. The Lord shows us how to plow, sow, plant, rotate, thresh, beat, and grind, to hammer, measure, and saw. And God can also show us how to build, manufacture, administer, study, analyze, nurture, choreograph, and portray. This teaching does not (necessarily) come from God directly appearing to us and pronouncing our task. Nor even is it (usually) given in the Bible. More commonly, God shows us our way by means of the creation itself. As the psalmist says:

> *The heavens are telling the glory of God;*
> *and the firmament proclaims his handiwork.*
> *Day to day pours forth speech,*
> *and night to night declares knowledge.*
> *There is no speech, nor are there words;*
> *their voice is not heard;*
> *yet their voice goes out through all the earth,*
> *and their words to the end of the world.*

Psalm 19:1–4

As we gaze at the starry heavens on a peerlessly clear night, pinpoints of light spread in numbers we cannot conceive. They are billions of miles distant, and they make our sun look like a pebble. As we realize that God made these in the blink of an eye, effortlessly, then we glimpse a little of God's majesty. As we realize that this is the same God who came to earth to live and die to save us, we catch a momentary glimpse of God's love. A night among the stars can be a seminar with God that no earthly teacher can touch.

Paul takes up this theme in Romans, saying that "what may be known about God is plain to them, because God has made it plain to them. . . . God's invisible qualities—his eternal power and divine nature—have been clearly seen, being understood from what has been made" (Rom. 1:19, 20). Preaching at Lystra, he describes the "rain from heaven and crops in their seasons" as God's witness (Acts 14:17). These texts are primarily concerned with emphasizing how the creation witnesses to and teaches about God himself. But they also show that whatever the creation genuinely teaches is a teaching from and by God.

Since God has made the world good, the way the world is made speaks to us of the will of its Creator. Even though twisted by sin, the creation has not lost its character as the expression of God's will. Whatever is genuinely of the creation, and not of sin, is a sign of God's will. The creation is an expression of God's will for us. And yet, it is God's Word that illuminates our way as we find his will for our lives.

GOD'S WORD, OUR LIGHT

God's Word is "a lamp to my feet and a light for my path" (Ps. 119:105). But a lamp is not something to be looked at. You don't buy a flashlight so you can stare at the bulb. The purpose of a lamp is not to illuminate itself but *other things*. Similarly, apart from its revelation of God, God's Word is meant to be a light on creation, helping us to see properly the world that God has made. It does not give great details about buildings, or marriages, or music, or physics. But in its light we can study the world and learn about such things. Indeed, since our minds have been darkened by sin, it is only in the light of God's Word that we can understand the creation aright (Rom. 1:20, 21).

God's Word is more than a light; it is a light *on a path*. It illuminates *the way before us*. If we walk at night we do not stare at our flashlight. Nor do we point it at the sky or at our feet. Rather we point it forward and down, hitting the ground about six feet ahead. We shine it on the path before us because *we want to see where we are going*. It illuminates the stones, cracks, gullies, and slopes so we know where to place our feet.

In the same way, as we study the Scriptures we need to shine them on the questions that lie before us on our pilgrimage. This includes not only questions concerning our personal life and the church, but also the farmer's questions of how and what to plant, or how to make our daily bread, and for all of us, how to deal with fields, factories, studies, and politics.

We need to study not only God's Word but also God's world; we study the world in the light of the Word. We need to study not only Isaiah but also industry. Not only Philemon but also politics. Not only Acts but arts. It is not for us to choose between knowing the Bible or the world; we need to *know the world biblically*.

This is what Christian schools or colleges are about, or should be about. Certainly they should teach the Bible. They should also teach arts, languages, sciences, and philosophy. But it is most important that they teach arts and languages and sciences in a way shaped by the Bible. If they do not do this, they serve little purpose.

CALLED TO CREATE, DEVELOP, AND ADAPT

One part of the essential teaching of Scripture is precisely the inescapable connections between human responsibility and human freedom. One essential part of being bound to the Word of God is that we are free to work out our service to God. As we have seen, there is a development of human life and society portrayed throughout the Scriptures. People continue to create new things. There is no reason to expect this cultural development to stop at the end of biblical revelation. Indeed, the command to fill the earth and bring forth fruit shows us that historical changes and development are very real, very much part of God's intention for human life.

We are called by God to create, to develop, and to adapt what is about us in response to the guidance that God has given us. As members of the body of Christ, we, like the original human family, are mandated by God. We too must take up our own task as shapers of the world. The nature of being human, of being made in the image of God, is that we are given responsibility for the earth. And real responsibility often comes when the answer is not obvious, when the laws and rules leave open several options, or when many different laws and rules apply at the same time. We are not just interpreters but also judges or deciders.

We have to make real decisions about how we can put flesh on what God has shown us to be the path of peace, hope, stewardship, and justice. God gives us real responsibility. Adam named the animals, and God accepted the names that Adam gave; Abraham argued with God about justice for Sodom and Gomorrah and appears to have won the argument. Our responsibility is both frightening and challenging. We cannot shrink from it.

FINDING THE BEST PATH FOR LEARNING

Many people, upon discovering that I studied both geology and politics, ask me, "What's the connection?" I usually answer,

"There is none, really." I simply did the one, stopped, and did the other. Of course we could find connections: the politics of mineral resources, for example. But for me, finding connections between the two disciplines was a fairly irrelevant concern. What was more interesting, and far more painful, was making the transition between the two disciplines.

I found my way into geology somewhat by accident. The English school system made us specialize early. Since my best grades were in the sciences, I was channeled into the science stream for my last three years of high school. Even then, I must have had some resistance to the sciences, since I juggled the timetable in order to do geography instead of chemistry.

Because English universities themselves were also highly specialized, students had to be admitted not only to the university itself, but also to a particular department and program. Students could only get into a department if they had taken the right set of high-school courses. My unusual school combination left me little choice but to enter geology or oceanography. And I didn't mind. I liked geology, as it freed me to do scientific work without being condemned to a life in the lab. I could pick up a hammer, pack, compass, and boots and head for the hills. Thus it was that a career path was laid for me by the time I became a Christian, just before heading off to university.

However, my conversion prompted a whole new set of thoughts and questions. I became interested in theology, in philosophy, and in society. I spent a lot of time reading and learning. After a couple of years, I found myself in the awkward situation of studying one thing in my classes during the day and something altogether different in the evening. I stayed in this pattern for a while and even started doctoral work in geology. But there were always two nagging worries: first, that I was competing against people who did geology not only during the day but also during the evening, so I could not possibly do as well. Second, if my real interests were pulling me away from my intended focus, could it be that I was not in the right field?

These tensions continued to grow over the years. I prayed and wavered back and forth. Sometimes I'd say, "I've got to switch fields." Then I'd ask myself, "How can you do that? You've put so many years into this. How can you 'waste' them?" Then I'd counter, "If I'm not doing the right thing, I'll only end up 'wasting' even more years."

This turmoil continued, punctuated by splendid times doing mineral exploration in the Canadian arctic—something that made me think I'd stay in geology, after all.

In the end, I decided to compromise by switching to philosophy of science so I could use my geological background. Yet deep down I knew that this half-measure would still leave me torn. So, on the first day of classes in my new term, I surprised even myself and enrolled in political theory. I completely switched fields, interests, and goals.

Is there a pattern in all of this? Is there something I can learn from it? Is there something I can teach? I don't think so; at least I can't find it, and I have tried for a long time. Are there some Christian rules that will tell us exactly what we should decide in circumstances like these? I don't think so, even after writing books about vocation. It's simply a case of prayerfully wrestling with all our God-given wits to discern the best path. Even then, there are no guarantees.

Our life's dance is not painted for us in footsteps on the floor. It's not laid out so we know where to place our next step. We simply have to judge which steps best fit the rhythms that we hear.

GOD'S WILL AND THE LAW

The mere fact that we are made in the image of God as responsible creatures shows that our task is not always fixed and predetermined with no room for freedom of implementation. We have to continually learn and apply the responsibility and freedom of decision that occurs *within the Bible itself.*

One aspect of our very real human responsibility and authority before God is in dealing with God's law. Perhaps the starkest example of this process takes place when Jesus is faced with the question of divorce. The Pharisees asked him: "Is it lawful for a man to divorce his wife for any and every reason?" (Matt. 19:3). Jesus answered that God had made man and woman to be one from the beginning of creation and so ". . . what God has joined together, let man not separate" (v. 6).

The Pharisees then asked, referring to Deuteronomy 24:4, why Moses commanded a certificate of divorce.

Jesus replied again, "Moses permitted you to divorce your wives because your hearts were hard. But it was not this way from the beginning" (Matt. 19:3–9).

Admittedly, it was Jesus himself who said this, and one could argue that Jesus could do things in relation to the law that we cannot. But Jesus was giving an example of how properly to read the law. He was saying that God, from the beginning of the creation, has put man and woman together, and he willed that they not be separated. But because sinful people could not manage to live with this complete restriction, Moses allowed them to divorce in order to avoid even worse problems.

In reading the law, Jesus went to God's basic intent ("from the beginning this was not so") and read the law given through Moses as a way of expressing this intent in a particular circumstance ("Moses allowed you"). Moses took the sinful situation into account and allowed divorce, but this did not mean that he thought God wanted marriage to be anything other than permanent.

Jesus corrected the Pharisees' interpretation of the law, and affirmed the permanence of marriage. But he did not even hint that Moses was wrong to make allowances for the sinful situation in which he lived. We have to work out the law in the most obedient way in the situation in which we live, but we should never think for a second that God's will for us has changed. God's intent has not varied, but laws must be made so as to give his intent its best expression. As John Calvin said:

> *The law of God given through Moses is (not) dishonored when it is abrogated and new laws are preferred to it . . . for the Lord . . . did not give that law to be proclaimed among all nations and to be in force everywhere. Rather we must make our laws with regard to the condition of times, place and nation. . . . How malicious and hateful toward public welfare would a man be who is offended by such diversity.*[2]

Calvin certainly did not think that God's law was only for Israel and only for that time. He did not think that we should ignore its teaching. But neither did he think that Old Testament law was supposed to be directly legislated for each and every country at every time. Rather, he taught that the law reveals God's will for us, which we must then try to implement in ways appropriate to our own country and time. He held that God's will was both absolute and also needed to be expressed in appropriate ways.

From this we can develop an understanding of how to read the law, and we can learn to give expression to God's law in the particular circumstances we are in. Indeed, the Mosaic law is not just a set of absolutes, but it also contains examples of its own application to particular situations.

The law is not just "principles" that we apply to our "particulars." Much of the Mosaic law is, itself, the working out of God-given principles in specific situations. The central principles are the Ten Commandments and, more so, the two great commandments quoted by Jesus, "'Love the LORD your God with all your heart and with all your soul and with all your mind.' This is the first and greatest commandment. And the second is like it: 'Love your neighbor as yourself'" (Matt. 22:37–39). These are the core standards that guide the rest of the law and must guide us in all our doings. Much of the rest of Deuteronomy is what lawyers would call "case law," law that takes a central principle and applies and works it out in particular cases. The law is to be developed and elaborated in terms of concrete circumstance.

This is not to say that God's commandment changes, but rather that the commandment must be expressed in such a way that its intent is fulfilled. The implementation of the law is always the implementation of God's abiding will in the specific and variable situations of our lives. Obviously, this can be a very difficult task, but this difficulty is itself a real reflection of our awesome human responsibility, and of course, for our need to continue to learn and grow. Whoever said it would be easy?

PRINCIPLES AND UNIVERSAL TRUTHS

Laws and principles provide the backbone and structure of how we live. Without them, we'd be left in the situation of infinite variability and situational ethics. But while we can never act obediently without them, neither can we act obediently if they are *all* we have. Principles are never themselves sufficient to give *all* the guidance we need. Apart from principles and absolutes, we need to know about particulars and concrete situations. While we should never for a second believe in situational ethics, we should never believe in ethics without situations.

For example, if we want to drive properly, we don't just need to learn about what cars are like, we also need to learn about *this* car. We don't just need to learn about highways, we also need to learn about *this* highway. If we want to train our dog, we don't just need to know about what dogs are like, we also need to know what *our particular* dog is like. If we want to knit a sweater, we don't just need to know what shape people are, we also need to know the shape of the person who is going to wear the sweater. We need to know about situations.

Similarly, if we want to govern a country, we don't need to know only about the Bible (though we need to), or only about countries in general (though we need to), we need to know about *this* country. If we want to make a law, we need to know about laws in general, including biblical laws, but we also need to know about *these* citizens, *this* legislature, *this* president, *this* constitution.

If principles and universal truths were sufficient to make laws or to run governments, we would no longer need personal judgment. But we also need people who have the skills, among other things, to make a judgment about a particular person or a particular city or a particular crime. Murder is wrong—always. But was *this* act murder? And, if so, was *this* person the murderer? We will never know this without the facts of the situation. This requires us to learn, to know and to make judgments about the infinite variabilities and idiosyncrasies of human life.

We must understand not only God's Word, but also God's world. We cannot, nor should we try to, find all the answers to all our questions in the Bible. While we can certainly use Christian principles to repair a car, none of us would want a mechanic who knows nothing but Bible texts. Good mechanics, Christian mechanics, must know the potentialities and the structure of an engine. They must know what a car is and how it works. And they must know about *this* car.

PLAYING BY THE RULES?

Perhaps another way of illustrating this is to say that God gives us the principles of the game—what the rules are and what the goals are. We cannot play any game, be it chess or basketball, without knowing the rules. However, simply knowing the rules is not enough to play. I know the rules of basketball, but nobody (I mean nobody) would choose me for a team.

Michael Jordan is not a great basketball player simply because he (usually) keeps the rules. He is a great player because he has learned what the possibilities are *within* the rules, and he has the skills to act out those possibilities. Merely knowing the foul rules or the free-throw rules does not teach us how to dribble, pass, or dunk. Rules tell us what we must do to win and what we can and cannot do. They give us our normative direction, the boundaries of our actions. *But we still have to learn to play*. We still have to discover and execute the billions of plays that are possible within the rules. Even a good referee can be a lousy player.

Similarly, we cannot fully appreciate all the complexities and potentialities of the "game," until we start to play. In art, politics, education, and work, the end result is not predetermined (except in the glorious final sense of Christ's ultimate victory and the renewal of all things). Our life always involves real questioning, probing, trying, learning, and revising as we struggle to learn and to do God's will in the situation at hand.

The Scriptures are not some divinely inspired *Encyclopedia Americana* wherein all human knowledge is found in godly form. They are not given to tell us everything but to show us the foundation of everything. They are focused on a particular message, the most important message in the world—on telling us who God is, who we are, how we came into being, what we live for, how and why we do evil and know suffering, and most especially how God has prepared and accomplished our salvation in Jesus Christ. This is the center and circumference of human life, by far the most important thing in human life—but it still remains our responsibility to learn what it means not only in our own lives but, throughout the creation.

And there is more. Learning is far more than a task or a responsibility. It also changes us. It fulfills our innate (that is, God-given) curiosity about the world. It is a way of increasing our sense of what life holds, therefore inspiring us to create. Learning heightens our ability to understand and sympathize. It broadens our perspective. It makes us richer, more mature people.

Ultimately, true learning also drives us back to rely more completely upon God because the more we learn, the more we realize how little we really know. The most profound learning ends in mystery. Real learning is the path to humility, trust, and faith. It can only be faithful learning and the learning of faith that directs us in the world. And this will reveal itself in our work.

A LEARNING MYSTERY

The drive from Telegraph Creek took longer than we had planned. The road was in rough shape; one of the bridges had washed out completely. Fortunately, the four-wheel drive managed to get us through, but by the time we crawled into the clearing where the helicopter would pick us up the next day, it was already long past dark. It was a remote site, so we simply took out the sleeping bags, collapsed on the ground, and called it a day.

The next morning started badly. We all were all jerked out of deep sleep at four o'clock by the bang of a shotgun. "Oh, no," I thought. "We're on someone's land. They're mad, and they're not the sort of people who'd bother to call in the (distant) police when they already have a shotgun."

It was only after hearing another blast a few seconds later, followed by the screeching sound of a flock of birds erupting from a nearby vegetable patch, that we concluded that the locals were not worried about invading geologists so much as invading crows.

Since we'd been awakened rather earlier than we'd hoped, and since we were well and truly awake, we wandered down to the banks of the Stikine to try to catch a glimpse of the salmon run. As we sat around, occasionally skimming stones, a boy came out of the woods. He was around eight years old and appeared to be all or part Indian. Even at that forbidding hour he was bright and alert.

He asked us what we did. We told him we were geologists and that we were off to do some exploration work near the Alaska border. The boy brightened up at this news and took me a little way down the river to look at some rocks. "Are these metamorphic rocks?" he asked.

I studied them for a while and said, "They might be, but I think they're just straight igneous."

He looked at them again and said, "I thought that, too, but they have these bands that have been twisted, so it didn't seem right."

We talked more about rocks, then about the river, the trees, the mountains, and the animals. He talked about them with all the knowledge of someone who had not only lived among them but had also studied them.

Before we left, I asked him what he did about schooling way out there. He said he had been to the nearest school but had dropped out. His teachers thought he was stupid.

six

A PERSPECTIVE ON WORK

Cal Seerveld, who knows more about work than anybody, tells how he learned from his father that all honest work is Christian ministry.

My father is a seller of fish. We children know the business too having worked from childhood in the Great South Bay Fish Market, Patchogue, Long Island, New York, helping our father like a quiver full of arrows. It is a small store, and it smells like fish.

I remember a Thursday noon long ago when my Dad was selling a large carp to a prosperous woman and it was a battle to convince her that the carp, "Is it fresh?"

It fairly bristled with freshness, had just come in, but the game was part of the sale. They had gone over it anatomically together: the eyes were bright, the gills were a good color, the flesh was firm, the belly was even spare and solid, the tail showed not much waste, the price was right—Finally my Dad held up the fish behind the counter, "Beautiful, beautiful! Shall I clean it up?"

And as she grudgingly assented, ruefully admiring the way the bargain had been struck, she said, "My, you certainly didn't miss your calling."

She spoke the truth. My father is in full-time service for the Lord, prophet, priest and king in the fish business. And customers who come in the store sense it. Not that we always have the cheapest fish in town! Not that there are no mistakes on a busy Friday morning! Not that there is no sin! But this: that little Great South Bay Fish Market, my father and two employees, is not only a clean, honest place where you can buy quality fish at a reasonable price with a smile, but there is a spirit in the store, a spirit of laughter, of fun, of joy inside the buying and selling that strikes an observer pleasantly; and the strenuous week-long preparations in the back rooms for Friday fish-day are not a routine drudgery interrupted by "rest periods," but again, a spirit seems to hallow the lowly work into a rich service, in which it is good to officiate.

When I watch my Dad's hands, big beefy hands with broad stubby fingers each twice the thickness of mine, they could never play a piano; when I watch those hands delicately split the back of a mackerel or with a swift, true stroke fillet a flounder close to the bone, leaving all the meat together; when I know those hands dressed and peddled fish from the handlebars of a bicycle in the grim 1930's, cut and sold fish year after year with never a vacation through fire and sickness, thieves and disaster, weariness, winter cold and hot muggy summers, twinkling at work without complaint, past temptations, struggling day in and day out to fix a just price, in weakness often but always in faith consecratedly cutting up fish before the face of the Lord: when I see that, I know God's Grace can come down to a man's hand and the flash of a scabby fish knife.[1]

Work is not the result of sin. It is a fact of creation, a gift from God. Work existed before the Fall, and the Bible says that it is one reason God made us. Since sin has come into the world, work has been corrupted. All too often it is painful not pleasant, frustrating not fulfilling. But it is still part of our calling, something we are meant to redeem. Work of any kind, from writing computer programs to changing diapers, can be a sacred task. And, as we shall see in later chapters, the challenges of our work and the fruits of our labor will continue even beyond the resurrection. The swords and the spears will be recast into plowshares and pruning hooks.

WHAT IS "WORK"?

The word *work* is not limited to situations of formal employment or to doing a certain job in order to earn a wage or salary. It certainly includes all these, but it also includes repairing the faucet, or helping the kids with their homework, or taking out the garbage, or making the bed. It includes church work, volunteer work, visiting the sick and prisoners, studying, and even certain types of prayer. It embraces any effort to shape and influence the world about us, including other people. Here I'll just concentrate on work that is usually regarded as "outside" of the church.

The Bible is full of praise for the work of human hands, hearts, and minds. Even God is described in terms of human work, as the one who makes, forms, builds, and plants the earth (Gen. 2:4, 7, 8, 19, 23). God is a worker. The craftsman Bezalel's artistry in wood and stone and jewels was given to him as he was filled with the Spirit of God (Exod. 35:30–32; see also Pss. 65:9–13; 104:22–24; Gen. 10:8–9). Craftsmanship is a gift of God so that we can image God the Worker. Nor is this a theme that disappears or diminishes in the New Testament. Here we find Jesus immersed every day in the life and problems of working people.

The apostles were mainly of humble background, and sometimes they returned to their work for a time even after being called by him. Jesus went off with them on fishing trips (Luke 5:1–10). He also worked as a carpenter for all but the last few years of his life. While he was on earth, Jesus probably spent more time sawing wood than he did preaching. His parables dealt with the working world, referring to sowers (Matt. 13:3), vineyard laborers (Matt. 13:30), harvesters (John 4:35), house builders (Matt. 7:24), swine tenders (Luke 15:11), and house keepers (Luke 15:8). He continually illustrated the kingdom of God by referring to the everyday work of those among whom he lived.

The Apostle Paul worked with his own hands so as not to be a burden to the church; he even worked to support others and urged this practice on other Christians (see 1 Thess. 4:11; 2 Thess. 3:6–10; Eph. 4:28). His advice to slaves—that they should work willingly as slaves of Christ—illustrates the same theme. It shows that he regarded even slave labor as potential service to the Lord on a par with his own work. Paul summarized his position in the remarkable assertion that "there is neither . . . slave nor free . . . you are all one in Christ Jesus" (Eph. 6:6–7; Gal. 3:28).

Similarly, his declaration "if anyone does not work, let him not eat" (2 Thess. 3:10) did not demonstrate callousness toward those who could not support themselves; his programs for deacons to serve those in need, collections on behalf of the poor, and sharing of goods show that this was not the case. Rather, Paul was focusing not on those who could not find work or were unable to work but on those who *could* but *refused* to share the burdens of others. His remarks were aimed at the Thessalonians who had become so obsessed with Jesus' Second Coming that they refused to work. They thought that they were too spiritual to be involved in such trivial, temporary, and worldly things. Paul's response has an edge of sarcasm; he implies that if they are so spiritual that they do not need to work, they must be so spiritual that they do not need to eat.

Paul continually asserted that a life given exclusively to leisure, religious contemplation, or end-times frenzy was a deficient life—that all members of the church should work. He didn't even make distinctions between physical and spiritual work. In fact he used exactly the same terms to refer both to the manual labor by which he earned a living and to his apostolic service.[2] Often it is quite difficult to know which one he was referring to or whether he himself had any interest in making such a distinction.

For Paul, all different types of work can originate in faith and are service to God. When he outlines the service of the "new self . . . created after the likeness of God," he urges "doing honest work with his hands." Clearly the new self, the new nature in Christ, is not some disembodied soul. The new self has hands and needs to use them! The new person restored in Christ is to work in God's world and to provide for the needs of others. Our new nature is, in this sense, intensely worldly.[3]

These New Testament principles are even more remarkable if we compare them to those of other cultures of that time. In high Greek culture, the manual worker was despised as one who was *forced* to do something; one who was bound by the necessities of life. Since the laborer *had* to work, he was something like a slave and so he was, in fact, considered a type of part-slave. For the Greek elite, the only life deemed worth living was a life freed from necessary work in order to pursue recreation, politics, philosophy or religion. The really free person did not have to work.[4]

In sharp contrast to this elitist view, Paul believed that true freedom did not come in release from work but from Christ. He did not regard philosophy or religion as "higher" than work. He did not even regard religion as an activity separate from our work. He regarded all aspects of life as equally religious and pleasing to God when faithfully done in service to God. He called upon Christians to manifest the image of God through their hands, bodies, minds, and hearts in day-to-day work.

One of the major features of the Protestant Reformation was a re-affirmation of this biblical doctrine of work. The Reformers did not regard a good Christian life as one that was confined solely to the church or to a particular "spiritual" realm. Medieval Catholic teaching had often elevated the contemplative life above all others so that monks and nuns and priests were the highest kind of Christians, and others were second class. By contrast, the Reformers emphasized the priesthood of all believers. This not only meant that we can all have direct access to God, but it also meant that all human service, all types of work, is equally service to God. We are all priests and prophets in our own task.

Martin Luther emphasized the goodness of everyday work, and he emphasized that the creation itself teaches us that this work is God's will. He stressed equally our responsibilities at home, taking special care so that men, husbands, and fathers got the point too. In his 1522 "Treatise on The Estate of Marriage," he declared that:

[When] natural reason—takes a look at married life, she turns up her nose and says, "Alas, must I rock the baby, wash its diapers, make its bed, smell its stench, stay up nights with it, take care of it when it cries, heal its rashes and sores, and on top of that care for my wife, provide for her, labor at my trade, take care of this and take care of that, do this and do that, endure this and endure that, and whatever else of bitterness and drudgery married life involves? What, should I make a prisoner of myself?

This is what natural reason thinks. It is, in the bad sense, worldly reasoning. But the new creature in Christ has a new life:

What then does Christian faith say to this? It opens its eyes, looks upon all these insignificant, distasteful, and despised duties in the Spirit, and is aware that they are all adorned with divine approval as with the costliest gold and jewels. It says, "O God, because I am certain that thou hast created me as a man and hast from my body begotten this child, I also know for a certainty that it meets with thy perfect pleasure. I confess to thee that I am not worthy to rock the little babe or wash its diapers, or to be entrusted with the care of the child and its mother. How is it that I, without any merit, have come to this distinction of being certain that I am serving thy creature and thy most precious will? O how gladly will I do so, though the duties should be even more insignificant and despised. Neither frost nor heat, neither drudgery nor labor, will distress or dissuade me, for I am certain that it is thus pleasing in thy sight. . . ."

Now you tell me, when a father goes ahead and washes diapers or performs some other mean task for his child, and someone ridicules him as an effeminate fool—though that father is acting in the spirit just described and in Christian faith—my dear fellow you tell me, which of the two is most keenly ridiculing the other? God, with all his angels and creatures, is smiling—not because a man is washing diapers, but because he is doing so in Christian faith.

Washing diapers, rocking babies, and making beds are "duties in the Spirit"; they are works of Christian faith. They bring joy to God and all the angels. This is part of the priesthood of all believers. Luther was not alone. One of the articles of supposed heresy for which William Tyndale, the great English Reformer and father of the English Bible, was convicted, accused him of having said: "There is no work better than another to please God: to pour water, to wash dishes, to be a *souter* [shoemaker] or an apostle, all is one; to wash dishes and to preach is all one, as touching the deed, to please God." For Tyndale, washing dishes was the spiritual equivalent of preaching, and shoemakers were as good as apostles (perhaps even better, if what you needed was shoes). All work, paid or unpaid, at home or in the field, can be a divine ministry.

THE RESTORATION OF WORK

Work is a gift of God. But we also know all too well that because we now live in a sinful world, work can seem anything but a gift. Some people cheapen the gift by selling it to the highest bidder. Others are so caught in a cycle of desperate poverty that they are driven to endless work. Work can be backbreaking and painful, boring and meaningless. This is not what God intended. But the solution to this is not to reject or despise work. It is to begin to live as new creatures in Christ to redeem working life, to fight sin and bring work closer to what God intended.

There are three things that we should keep in mind where work is concerned. First, we should affirm that all genuine human tasks are equally God-given and are equally spiritual. Obviously, at times some things are more urgent and have priority over others, but no one type of human activity can claim a basic spiritual priority over another. We must echo Tyndale's declaration that "to wash dishes and to preach is all one, as touching the deed, to please God," and we must reject the sub-Christian view of work that has pervaded much of the Christian church and especially its evangelical wing. We human beings are not simply waiting to get out of this world. We are those whom God has made to tend the earth and serve one another through our everyday work. While sin continues to cause pain and frustration, work has not lost its essential character as service to Creator and creature.

Second, work must not be regarded as the antithesis of human fulfillment. We are not creatures destined for a life of freedom from work but somehow trapped in an ungodly cycle of duty and necessity. Instead, we are called to manifest the image of God and, hence, to be free, precisely in and through our work, in and through the daily necessities of life. We must oppose the opinion of our society that elevates certain professions in the fields of medicine, law, or engineering while treating other types of work as something to be minimized if at all possible. It can fairly be said that modern society underestimates (as well as overestimates) work.

As Sander Griffioen notes, modern culture treats work as "a condition for the development of the individual, rather than being part of this development."[5] But personal fulfillment was never intended to be something we pursue *after* work; it can be, and God intends it to be, part of work. Pope John Paul II well expresses a Christian "theology of work" when he emphasizes that work is an essential part of any genuine human development: "For when a man works he not only alters things and society, he develops himself as well. He learns much, he cultivates his resources, he goes outside of himself and beyond himself. Rightly understood, this kind of growth is of greater value than any external riches which can be garnered."[6]

Third, we must live out the fact that work is the act of a creature made in the image of God. Consequently work should be, as much as we can make it, an action of responsibility carried out by a free image-bearer of God. This also contrasts with many of the dominant patterns in our society. An understanding of work as an activity reflecting the image of God necessarily makes us realize the importance of human responsibility as well as the theme of human freedom. We must concentrate not only on money and wages as "compensation" for work (though, of course, all people have a right to be sustained in and through their work) but on making work a genuine reflection of our faith as well.

As R. H. Tawney emphasizes, this is necessary for any good economic order: "Both the existing economic order, and too many of the projects advanced for reconstructing it, break down through their neglect of the truism that, since even quite common men have souls, no increase in material wealth will compensate them for arrangements which insult their self-respect and impair their freedom."[7] The question is not just how much we get paid but also how faithful we are to use our gifts and how responsible we can be to shape things that genuinely help our fellow human beings.

PRICELESS WORK

It was good to be back in Hazelton. The last time had been in deep winter—minus 35°—and the cold mist hanging over the village had been suffused with pink tones as the setting sun glanced back from the overarching peaks of the Seven Sisters. I had to be careful not to hit moose on the highway as I drove in.

On this trip, there was less time to admire the scenery; I was seeking to make contact with a famous Indian carver. After several inquiries, I managed to find the house where Jim O'Malley lived (lots of the Gitskan-Wetsuweten Indians have Irish names—it's a long story).

At the door, Jim was a little shy about inviting me in until he learned that I'd brought a message from his brother-in-law. We sat in the kitchen and talked—in that culture, it's very impolite to quickly settle down to business as though you didn't care who the other person was. You need to know who you're dealing with.

Jim could carve almost anything, from rings he engraved with a diamond drill to towering Douglas firs he shaped with an axe. He was most famous for his totem poles, and as we talked I learned that he had poles in museums in Vancouver and Victoria as well as in Amsterdam, Paris, and Frankfurt.

Despite the way they appear to many Europeans, totem poles are not idols or objects of worship. It's hard to translate them into our terms, but in a way they are tribal or family histories. They set down important events and provide aids to telling the story of the past. And, while they are not cultic objects, neither are they to be taken lightly. They are serious cultural symbols, not to be confused with mere decorations.

Something about this subject was clearly troubling to Jim, and eventually he described a visit he'd had that morning from two American theme park executives. They were designing hotels and, since each of their hotels had individual motifs, they wanted to develop a Northwest coast one, which they wanted flanked by totem poles. After checking around, they'd decided Jim was their man. They had flown into Smithers, picked up a truck, and eventually negotiated the dirt road to the village. And they had asked Jim to carve two poles for the hotel entrance.

Jim had been somewhat impressed by the fact that they had at least wanted real poles, but still it was not a project with which he felt comfortable. Totem poles were not hotel decorations. He explained to them that poles this large would require trees to be brought in from the Queen Charlotte Islands. The logs would need to be transported by boat, and then on individual logging trucks, and finally be laid out behind his house before he could even begin work. This was an expensive process.

The executives didn't seem perturbed by these hints of great cost, so Jim decided to decline their offer in a very polite way. He thought of a high price for the finished poles, multiplied it by ten, and quoted this figure to the Americans.

But, without flinching, they just said, "Okay."

Jim was a little puzzled by this and, since he was a man of his word, he was also a little trapped. He had little choice but to carve the poles as promised, and in return he would receive an enor-

mous paycheck. He was amazed by the episode. He was vaguely regretful, too, as if he might have betrayed something in the process.

WORK: A PURPOSE OR A PAIN?

The redemption of our work requires from us a renewed sense of vocation and a willingness to rejoice in being servants. Our work is a means of giving good things and services to others: it is a means of meeting human (and non-human) needs. But work and responsibility is not intended to bring about merely our own personal renewal. John Donne's observation that "no man is an island" applies to our work life as well. For most of us, work does not depend merely on our own commitment and motivations; it depends also on the attitudes, motivations, and actions of others, especially of those who came before us and who have shaped the situation in which we work.

When we go to the factory or office, field or school, most of us are not in charge of the way we work. We don't set the hours, we don't divide the responsibilities, we don't establish the goals. Usually we're just supposed to fit in with what is already there, with someone else's plan and vision. The attitudes of others have already been built into the factories, offices, schools, and workplaces we have designed, the types of products we manufacture, the types of machines we work with, and the rhythm and pace of our work itself.

Individuals in an auto plant conceivably can have a strong sense of their vocation to make good, relatively cheap cars that people will be happy to drive. But it is almost impossible to maintain such a sense if all you do is endlessly screw in the same kind of bolts on an auto assembly line amid howling noise. In fact, in this type of situation a sense of vocation may be out of place because it is out of touch with reality. Often people are not being treated as responsible people, as image-bearers of God. They are not being allowed to serve their neighbor. For them, work is being diminished as a calling and has become a pain.

The biblical picture of work as responsibility to God implies that those of us that can must seek to restructure work so that it can really and honestly be an expression of our service and calling. We need to shape our workplaces and organizational structures so that people can exercise genuine responsibility and be treated as God's responsible image-bearers. This means we should concentrate on good, useful work and turn away from the notion that people are simply commodities to be bought and sold in a "labor" market. As much as we can, we should seek to help ourselves and others find and shape work as an act of responsibility, a genuine way of serving our neighbor and of serving God.

Human responsibility is key not only to fulfilling work but also to good economics. Management consultants such as Peter Drucker have emphasized that a key even to monetary success in a modern economy is to treat people like human beings. People want to contribute if we will let them. Their good work becomes a reflection of human friendship and companionship.

John Calvin's view of economic activity reflects this pattern of responsibility and mutual servitude. For him, commerce was a natural way for people to relate to and commune with one another.

It is not enough when one can say, "Oh, I work, I have my trade, I set the pace." This is not enough; for one must be concerned whether it is good and profitable to the community and if it is able to serve our neighbours . . . And this is why we are compared to members of a body. The life of the Godly is justly compared to trading, for they ought naturally to exchange and barter with one another in order to maintain intercourse.

Our membership in the body of Christ and in the whole world is to be shown not only in the church but also in the home, the factory, the school, the field, the office, and the voting booth. All of these are divine gifts. We need one another's gifts, and we need one another's work; they are part of our service to God.

BRINGING HEAVEN INTO THE WORKPLACE

One way in which we might demonstrate this service is in the way we commission people in our churches. Usually, if people decide to go to seminary, if they enter the pastorate, or if they go off to mission fields, we call them before the congregation, pray for them, commend them to the Lord, and commit ourselves as a congregation to remember them and support them. This is good; we should keep on doing it.

But we should not stop here. If all genuine work is a divine ministry, we should commission all workers. When members of our church become doctors, or nurses, or lawyers, or teachers, or members of Congress; when they become bricklayers, police officers, or forest rangers, let us call them forward and commission them as well. We must let them know that they are doing a service to the Lord and to their neighbors and that we will stand with them and pray for them and support them.

When young people go to university, engineering school, computer training, secretarial school, or heavy machinery training, let us commend them to God. When teenagers begin their first jobs working at McDonald's or delivering papers or serving as lifeguards, let us pray with them to God as they begin their servanthood.

All these are God's servants, doing God's will. They are certainly God's ambassadors, witnessing to Jesus Christ wherever they are placed. But this is not only a matter of explicit evangelism. They are also God's ambassadors because they are called by God to be diligent, careful, cheerful, and caring workers, regardless of their trade.

Often, non-believers have really had it up to here with Christians. The evangelical who slips talk about Jesus into every conversation becomes a pain and a bit of a joke. But the worker who does his or her job diligently, cheerfully, and well is a walking testimony worth a thousand words. People watch us. If we are people worth imitating, people will want to imitate us. If we show a life worth following, people will want to follow that course of life.

But we do not work only to evangelize. Our work *itself* is a divine service to others. We get sick, we drive on roads, we read newspapers, we eat hamburgers: those who provide for us are God's servants, whether they know it or not. Let us take this awareness of service, and this deeper appreciation of work, into our congregations, into our lives, and into our hearts.

When Adam thus to Eve: "Fair consort, the hour
Of night, and all things now retired to rest,
Mind us of like repose; since God hath set
Labour and rest, as day and night to men
Successive, and the timely dew of sleep
Now falling with soft slumbrous weight inclines
Our eyelids; other creatures all day long
Rove idle, unemployed, and less need rest;
Man hath his daily work of body or mind
Appointed, which declares his dignity,
And the regard of Heaven on all his ways".[8]

R̄EFLECTIONS ON REST

In the plain basement of an industrial town, I looked out over a roomful of alert but tired people. At that time, St. Catherines, Ontario, had one of the largest percentages of General Motors employees in Canada, and the making of auto parts remains a major industry there. These people had probably rushed to this meeting after a quick meal, or perhaps after no meal at all. I had dashed to the lecture from my last class of the day, fighting the rush hour traffic on the highway for an hour and a half, and was already feeling wiped out.

These women and men were members of the Christian Labour Association of Canada, an organization of Christians who work in union occupations in factories, nursing homes, construction sites, and supermarkets, united in trying to bring a communal Christian witness to everyday work. Since my audience was comprised mainly of Dutch Calvinists, who are famous for their disciplined work habits, I had been invited to speak on "A Christian View of Work."

The talk was going quite well when, near the end, I strangely and inexplicably ad libbed a few comments on the topic of rest (maybe I was tired). My comments were very short, since I knew almost nothing about the subject myself. A one-hour question period then followed. Despite the work-oriented focus of my talk, every question, every comment, every story shared by the audience was on rest—or rather, on a lack of it.

For these earnest, dedicated, hard-working people, who know perhaps better than any other Christians that everyday work is our Christian vocation, the many struggles of life now seemed to center not around the virtues of work but around how to find rest.

"How can I rest when there are still so many things to do?"

"When I get home from work, I've got an elders meeting at church on Monday. I've got a meeting at the Christian school on Tuesday. I go to the prayer meeting on Wednesday. Thursday I try to do my finances so they won't get in the way of being at the young people's meeting on Friday or doing house repairs on Saturday."

"When I rest I feel guilty. Actually, since I am a Calvinist, when I work I feel guilty too. But I feel more guilty when I rest."

I struggled with these comments and questions, since I was in exactly the same boat as the audience. I had unwittingly posed a question for which none of us had the answer, and I had no idea what to do with it.

Resting is no small matter. It is not simply flaking out when everything else is done. In fact, rest is at the heart of our relationship with God and is a fundamental reflection of our faith. Rest is close to the heart of faith. Under God, we find our ultimate fulfillment not in what we achieve, but in freely receiving what God has freely given, what God has achieved.

WORK'S RIGHTEOUSNESS?

We are strange creatures. Most of us manage to not only have problems with work but also problems with rest, and often both of them right at the same time. We not only downplay the place of work in God's kingdom; we downplay rest as well.

We sometimes forget that though work is a good thing, it is not the *only* thing, nor even the greatest thing. We are not saved by work any more than we are saved by works. This is not some abstract theological point; this truth lies at the very heart of the Gospel. Since our relation with God is what ultimately shapes our lives and the world itself, it also means that we cannot achieve genuine wealth or happiness or security or peace through our work. Jesus praised work, but he also sharply limited it. The parable of the two sons (usually called the Prodigal Son) emphasizes how we are accepted by God's love not by our own diligence or lack of it (see Luke 15:11–32).

In the parable, the younger son grasped at his inheritance then wasted it on parties and hookers. And yet he was still received back with joy by his father. However, the story is not about one son but two. It is also about the older brother. This other son had never demanded his inheritance. He had stayed home and faithfully worked, obeyed, and been a dutiful son.

All the thanks he seemed to get for these years of service was to be ignored while everyone else had a big feast for his wastrel brother. Nobody had even told him about the party: he was simply left out in the field and only learned about the celebration when he came back to the house after a long day. He was then so angry that he wouldn't even go in. His father had to come out and plead with him to join them.

The elder son complained (with real justification, as far as I can see), "Look! All these years I've been slaving for you and never disobeyed your orders. Yet you never gave me even a young goat so I could celebrate with my friends. But when this son of yours, who has squandered your property comes home, you kill the fattened calf" (vv. 29–30).

The elder brother is often dumped on in sermons, commentaries, and Bible notes. He's treated as selfish and conceited. And yet, didn't he have a valid complaint? What would we have done in the same circumstance? If we worked faithfully, while our brother wasted everything, how would we feel when he got the party? We would hit the roof, you can bet. I would. The elder son may well be meant to represent the Pharisees—but he represents all of us, and all too well.

What do we think of people who slack off while we slave away? "*He's* on welfare. *We* are decent, hard-working people who never asked for a dime." "*He* hangs around with prostitutes. *We* are faithful." "*He* blew his money. *We* saved carefully." Of course we say in our theology that works don't bring God's grace. We say that we are all equally sinners and all equally undeserving in the eyes of God. But doesn't there still lurk in our hearts the belief that work and duty really do count for something, that they are really what it's all about? According to Jesus, God doesn't think so.

Jesus demolishes our view all over again in his parable of the vineyard laborers (Matt. 20:1–16). In this vineyard some started working "early in the morning" (probably at about 6 A.M.). Others were hired at the third hour, then the sixth hour, then the ninth hour. Some were even hired at the eleventh hour (about 5:00 P.M.). All of them quit work at exactly the same time, but they all got paid exactly the same. The people who had worked in the heat all day complained that others had only worked for an hour, and in the cool of the evening, too. Let's not dump on them either. We would complain if this happened to us. I certainly would. In fact, I still do.

The purpose of these parables is not to tell us how we should treat our relatives or how we should pay people. Nor are the stories meant to denigrate work: we've already seen that work is good. Instead, Jesus' words are focused on pounding home to us the fact that God's grace is given freely, which means *it is not earned.* This is the point. It is not work that brings grace, nor even the fruits of grace: *they are God's gifts.* We need to know this deeply in our hearts before we can ever begin to rest. Some of the most radical words we can say to our society, and to ourselves, are:

> *Do not be anxious about your life, what you shall eat or what you shall drink. . . . Consider the lilies of the field, how they grow; they neither toil nor spin. . . . But if God so clothes the grass of the field, which today is alive and tomorrow is thrown into the oven, will he not much more clothe you, O men of little faith?* [1]

All of our work and effort and pain will not clothe us like the lilies. But God will, and freely.

WHEN WORK BECOMES IDOLATRY

The Scriptures not only reject salvation by works, but they also condemn excessive pride in work. The sin of Adam and Eve, that they wished to be gods, was replayed in the construction of the tower of Babel "with its top in the heavens." Babel expresses a lust for achievement and greatness that rejects God's limits and so only ends up driving people apart from each other (Gen. 11:1–9). Isaiah repeats this theme. "For the Lord of hosts has a day against all that is proud and lofty, against all that is lifted up and high . . . against every high tower, and against every fortified wall. . . . And the haughtiness of man shall be humbled, and the pride of men shall be brought low; and the Lord alone will be exalted in that day" (Isa. 2:12–17).

Excessive pride in our own achievements becomes idolatry, which, as we will see in chapter 13, is worship—placing final trust in anything within creation, and especially final trust in the work of our own hands. *The workman trusts in his own creation* when he makes dumb idols" (Hab. 2:18–19). As Paul warned the people of Athens, God is not like the idols, which are only "like gold, or silver, or stone, *a representation by the art and imagination of man*" (Acts 17:29; see also Rom. 1:24).

If we worship idols with our lives, if we worship our own work, skill, and achievement, we in turn will start to become like what we worship. As the psalmist says: "The idols of the nations are silver and gold, *the work of men's hands.* They have mouths, but they speak not, they have eyes, but they see not, they have ears, but they hear not, nor is there any breath in their mouths. *Those that trust in them are like them!* Yea, so is every one that trusteth in them (Ps. 135:15–18, KJV, emphasis added in each text).

If we trust in the wrong things, if we worship that which has not life, we will remake ourselves as people who cannot speak, cannot see, cannot hear, and cannot breathe. This is what happens to us when we trust in and so become obsessed with our work. These are the symptoms of the workaholic.

Those who are obsessed with their work shut out all those around them. They cannot see or hear or speak because their attention is completely focused on their own projects and endeavors. They exclude all other interests, interruptions, and activities. They cannot breathe, suffocated by their fixation on performance, perfectionism, and productivity. They are preoccupied, unable to rest, seized with frantic activity. Perhaps above all else, they want to be in control of their lives.

Their responsibilities may involve good and honest causes, even "Christian" or "ministry" jobs. Pastors are often the worst workaholics. But, whatever their work, good or bad, the key is that workaholics are *addicted* to their work. And, as we will see in a later chapter, addiction is a form of idolatry. In this case, workaholism destroys the ability of its victims to enjoy wholesome or intimate relationships with other people. Even more tragically, it keeps them at a remote distance from a genuine relationship with God.

As Wayne Oates explains, "Far from thinking of God as someone who loves us whether we produce or not, this is unthinkable to workaholics. Acceptance is pay for work done."[2] And, as Paul Stevens says, "Workaholics do not work because they have a desire to be gainfully employed; they work to prove something to themselves. Though they keep trying by working harder, working better or trying to find the perfect job, they can never do enough to give full meaning to their lives."[3]

I once received a phone call from Christianity Today, *asking me if I would write an editorial for them. Since I was away from Toronto and working in Vancouver at the time, they'd had some difficulty in reaching me, and they were in a hurry.*

> *The editorial was to be centered on a recent book,* The Over-worked American, *which revealed how North Americans were now working longer hours than we had ten, twenty, or thirty years ago, even though Europeans were working shorter hours. I was asked to focus the article on how and why we seem to be ever more overworked and how difficult we find it to rest.*
>
> *They managed to get hold of me late on a Friday. I asked them when they wanted the article. In a display of stunning hypocrisy, they said, "Monday."*
>
> *In an even greater display of hypocrisy, I simply said, "O.K."*

Because we are to worship God rather than idols, we must find our true end in what God has given, not in what we can achieve, not in work but in grace. Our eyes are always meant to be on him, the one who provides all things for us.

Many women and men struggle to survive financially and are burdened with heavy fiscal responsibilities. They are forced to work long and hard. But it does not add to our financial burdens to remember that Jesus has called us to absolute dependence upon him. This does not mean that we stop working, stop trying, stop caring. But it does mean that we must entrust our financial concerns to him and not immerse ourselves in work simply because we are obsessively afraid of humiliation or financial disaster.

REST, FROM GOD'S PERSPECTIVE

We should be guided by ways to be followed rather than goals to be achieved. No matter what our circumstances, we should pay heed to Jesus' admonitions in the Sermon on the Mount:

So do not worry, saying, "What shall we eat?" or "What shall we drink?" or "What shall we wear?" For the pagans run after all these things, and your heavenly Father knows that you need them. But seek first his kingdom and his righteousness, and all these things will be given to you as well. Therefore do not worry about tomorrow, for tomorrow will worry about itself. Each day has enough trouble of its own.

Matthew 6:31–34

The things that Jesus tells us not to be anxious about are not bad things. They are good things. They are things we need and ought to have. But he says that being anxious for them, striving for them, will not help. Instead we are told to seek first the kingdom of God, and the other things will follow.

Jesus' words are a direct rebuke to every kind of idolatry. He does not set forth new goals but prescribes a way for us to follow that daily seeks his will, and he promises that God's blessing will flow from our diligence. *Blessing is not the result of work. It is the fruit of obedience.* Our lives are not guaranteed of success. They are not even to be oriented to success. Instead they are taking up a prayerful path of obedience to God in the problems that confront us, hour by hour, and decade by decade.

As creatures made in the image of God, we are called to do many things other than our jobs. We are called to be Christianly responsible *in all* our relationships: we are to be good husbands, wives, parents, children, neighbors, friends, and citizens. Our calling is to reflect God's image in every dimension of our existence—including worship, intimacy, play, and rest. While rest, meditation, and contemplation are not a higher kind of life, they are an essential part of our life. Our work has no prior claim, per se,to our time. As Thomas Aquinas says, "The essence of virtue consists in the good rather than in the difficult."[4]

REST AS AN ACT OF TRUST

One part of our calling is the calling to rest. Even God rested after creating the world. The commandment not to labor on the Sabbath carries as much weight as the commandments not to kill or steal. During the time of exile in the wilderness, Israel was promised rest in the land (see Deut. 3:20; Jer. 46:27), a rest that was also a respite from their enemies (see Deut. 3:10; 2 Sam. 7:11). Israel's life was ordained as a rhythm of work and rest. Each seventh day, each seventh year, and each seven of seven years was to be a Sabbath for people, for animals, and for the land itself.

This ordained cycle of work and rest was intimately tied to Israel's trust in God. If the Israelites rested in the seventh year, they would not plant and they would have no crops, and they needed to trust God's promise that the land would produce a surplus to see them through (Lev. 25:18–24). In the fiftieth year, the year of Jubilee, Israel's faith was tested even more. As the people celebrated the Day of Atonement they needed to put aside planting for two whole years; they would have to live off the gifts of God (Lev. 25:8–12). If God was not faithful, they might starve or have to sell themselves back into Egypt. Rest was always an act of trust, of faith. Similarly, the New Testament often pictures salvation as entering into rest, as trusting and receiving God's gifts (Heb. 3–4). And Jesus himself promised the freedom of rest to those who came to him.

This biblical picture of rest can be contrasted with the industrialized world's drive to escape from work. We manufacture distractions and entertainment; we live for Friday and Saturday nights; we count days to vacations. These activities simply try to ignore and negate work and, hence, are actually controlled by it. Our most characteristic "leisure activity" is consumption—buying things—an activity that, through the manufacture of "life styles," has become ever more hectic and more akin to work.

Perhaps as a result, our society finds itself increasingly distant from real rest. Its artificial "holidays" (including "Labor Day") are becoming mere excuses for novel forms of consumption. It is the malls that tell us when the holidays are. The notion of a Sabbath rest, or even of Sunday, is shouldered aside not only as an affront to the secular belief that God is irrelevant to social life but also, in what amounts to perhaps the same thing, as an obstruction to the drive to consume more.

Biblically, rest is far more than recuperation from and preparation for work, though certainly we do need to recuperate. It is a God-given human response in its own right. As Josef Pieper says, "It is not simply the result of external factors, it is not the inevitable result of spare time, a holiday, a week-end or a vacation. It is . . . a condition of the soul."[5]

Indeed, rest and work may involve similar activities but activities done in a different spirit. For me, reading is a part of work and a part of rest. The question is not about the activity itself but about the orientation of our hearts. Resting is intimately tied to faith—which is one reason why most of us avoid it. It is also why medieval Christendom so often pictured it as a higher way. The

Scriptures frequently relate lack of rest to unbelief (see Ps. 95:8–11; Heb. 3:7–4:10).

When we rest, we acknowledge that all our striving will, of itself, do nothing. Rest means letting the world pass us by for a time. Genuine rest requires acknowledging that God and our brothers and sisters can survive without us. It requires recognizing our own insufficiency and handing over responsibility. It is truly surrendering to the ways of God. It is a moment of celebration, when we acknowledge that blessing comes only from the hand of God. This is why rest requires faith. It is also why salvation can be pictured as rest. When we rest we accept God's grace: we do not seek to earn; we receive. We do not justify; we are justified.

"GOD DOTH NOT NEED . . . MAN'S WORK"

John Milton, one of the great giants of the English language, was an enormously productive man in his first forty years. Along with his prolific writings, both political and literary, during the course of his life, he apparently read nearly everything that existed in English, Latin, Greek, and Italian. He knew the Bible by heart. When Milton was still a young man, his indulgent father sent him to Europe for two years simply to visit and learn from the Continent's famous literary figures. He also worked at the center of English politics.

Then, during his forties, Milton lost his eyesight. His entire career had revolved around the written word, and there was no Braille. Although he was able to dictate both political pamphlets and his poems Paradise Lost *and* Paradise Regained, *his life seemed robbed of its former enthusiasm, freedom, and, to his mind, productivity. In reflection, he wrote a sonnet, which power-fully portrays the turmoil that blindness wrought in his soul. He describes man's desire to please God with work, which he then contrasts with God's desire that people serve him simply by sub-mitting to his will.*

Milton concludes,

. . . "Doth God exact day-labour, light denied?"
I fondly ask. But Patience, to prevent
That murmur, soon replies: "God doth not need
Either man's work or his own gifts; who best
Bear his mild yoke, they serve him best. His
state is kingly: thousands at his bidding speed,
And post o'er land and ocean without rest;
They also serve who only stand and wait."

eight

THE PLEASURES OF PLAY

On the west end of the island of Mull in Scotland's Inner Hebrides lies the village of Bunessan. Not many people stop there—most hurry farther on to catch the ferry to the island of Iona with its ancient abbey and stories of Celtic Christianity.

Our geology class did stop, however. We spent the days hiking and hammering rocks and, in the evenings, went back to the Bunessan Arms Inn for dinner, chatter, and bed.

One night, one of the waitresses mentioned that some of the "local lads" wanted to know if we'd like to have a soccer game. We did. It was decided we'd have one the following night. Next day, we tried, to no avail, to prevail upon our professors not to make us climb too many mountains since we were meant to be performing at our athletic best that night. Following a hard day of work, we went back to the inn, had a quick bite to eat, then drove up a winding rocky road to the hillside behind the village.

There we got something of a shock. The "local lads" turned out to be the village soccer team. They wore matching uniforms, and their team included the local policemen and firemen, who were rather large Scottish gentlemen of a size one wouldn't feel like tackling after a hard day's work in the mountains of Mull. Another shock was that it seemed the entire village had shown up to watch the game. There were about 200 cheering spectators on the sidelines.

Yet another shock was the pitch itself. The Hebrides are rocky islands, and it would be hard to find a level place there. I'd wondered during the daytime how the village had found a flat place to play soccer. The answer was easy. They hadn't. The pitch tilted from west to east. The ground also rolled slightly in undulating waves and, in at least one place, there was a large outcrop of rock.

The sun was going down, so we were expecting a short game. This hope, however, was changed by the fact that the cars parked on the sidelines were all facing inward, and the locals simply resorted to the expedient of switching on their headlights. And, since there were only ten of us, we started the game with only ten people on our team.

It was an evening both crazy and magical. Part of the craziness was that, since the field was lit by headlights shining horizontally at a height of three feet, everybody cast shadows that stretched across the pitch. You had to remember not to pass the ball to someone on your right, because in order to get it, that person would be looking straight into the headlights, unable see a thing. Most of the time, simply trying to see the ball was like trying find a flyball coming straight out of the sun.

As the game progressed and we were getting pounded by the "lads," we started to learn local techniques, such as bouncing the ball off the rocky outcrop near the middle of the pitch. Since the *pitch was uneven, we began to lose players to twisted ankles. But it turned out that the really dangerous part came when, if chasing a ball near the sidelines, you actually ran off the pitch. If you did this on the side where the crowd was gathered, the danger was not in running into a players' bench, or into the crowd, but in barreling into the front of one of the cars parked two feet beyond the line. And this was the safe side of the pitch.*

The other side was swamp and heather and rocks. At one point in the game, we realized that one of our players was missing. And, though this isn't strictly allowed in soccer, we did manage to call a time out in order to locate the missing person. We got into a huddle with the other team to try to remember the last time anybody had last seen Ralph. Someone recalled that he had chased the ball to the heather side of the pitch and had just managed to keep it in play. We ran over to the spot and discovered that his momentum had taken him careening into the heather, whereupon he had stuck his foot down a rabbit hole. His foot had stayed where it was, but the rest of his body had carried on forward. The result was a broken leg. We found him lying unconscious on a comfortable pillow of purple-scented heather.

We suggested eagerly that maybe we should end the game there, but the referee suggested a solution. As the local ambulance driver was on the other team, he could take Ralph to the hospital, and so the teams would remain relatively even in number. I think we lost one other person in the heather that night, though his injuries were not so drastic. We finished the game with six people still standing, losing by the not-too-upsetting score of 3–1.

While this mayhem took place on the field, the surrounding landscape changed mystically in the evening light. Below us was the ocean, and in the distance, before the setting sun, lay a string of silhouetted islands including Iona and the legendary island of Staffa, home of Fingal's Cave. Across an inlet lay the flattened peak of Ben Mhor. It carried a cap of white cloud that continually poured over the cliff edges and slowly dissolved in purple splendor as it slid down toward the sea. About halfway through the game, these clouds glowed a brilliant red in the setting sun, even as stars were twinkling overhead.

The magic was not only in the surrounding beauty but also in the event itself, in its sheer craziness. We went back to the village, gathered at the inn with what seemed like the entire population, and regaled the night away. Before we had limped into the inn, we'd been saying, never again, ever. But at some point in the festivities, in the early hours of the morning, when the innkeeper asked if we wanted to do it again, we said sure. We did.

Play is one of our highest callings as Christians. So much else in our lives is properly taken up in doing things—*things we do to change things, things we do in order that something else may happen.* But in play we are not seeking to change anything, nor are we seeking something beyond. We are simply being at home in the world and at peace with God.

RULES ABOUT REST AND PLAY

We need to learn, work, and rest, and we need to play. In one sense, this may be wrongly stated—for play is a kind of rest. This is true not only of seemingly relaxing games but also for the most strenuous ones. A game of basketball or a game of chess can wear out body and mind so that we can hardly drag ourselves off the court or away from the board. But despite our tiredness, we feel invigorated. It has not been work, though we've sweated. It has not been an ordeal, though we've concentrated hard. Rather than feeling drained, however, we will be, after a time of rest, even more rested and renewed for the challenges that await us in a new day or a new hour.

Sometimes it's very hard to know how to distinguish between work and play. At first glance, the difference seems obvious, but if we delve deeper, all the lines seem to blur. One person's play can be another one's work. Some people fly planes for a living; other people fly planes for fun. Some people repair cars for a living; other people repair cars for fun. Some people garden for a living; other people garden for fun. It's not the activity itself that makes the difference between work and play, or even rest. It's the spirit in which we engage in them.

At the meeting in St. Catherine's where I spoke on "A Christian View of Work," this point was starkly underscored. During the question period when we were talking about rest, one of the people in the audience asked if it was all right to garden on the Sabbath. I was about to answer that, as far as I could tell, it was fine. But then I remembered that this was also an agricultural area, with vineyards, orchards, and market gardens.

"What do you do for a living?" I asked him.

He smiled. "I'm a market gardener."

The answer was clear. "No, it's not all right for you to garden on the Sabbath, even in your own back garden. It's okay for your auto mechanic neighbors to do it, but not for you. Do something different."

What is the spirit that distinguishes play? It's quite simple, though profound. *Play is what we do for no reason at all. Play is not done for any reason outside of itself. It is done for its own sake.*

At first this may seem terrifying and even blasphemous to us. There's so much to do. Who in this cold, cruel, difficult, and suffering world can justify playing? Well, the answer is almost everybody. Even those people who are almost destitute or otherwise distressed will usually play when they can.

My last book, *Their Blood Cries Out*, discusses the persecution of Christians around the world in the 1990s. It describes people being beaten, raped, imprisoned, tortured, and killed. But even these people play when they can. People around the world, even the poorest, are never satisfied to dress in plain, old clothes; they'll add color or style in any way they can. In a similar way, people will enliven their lives with playfulness whenever they find the opportunity.

Of course, there are people in prison, there are people who are starving, there are people in severe physical pain, and there are people limited in any number of other ways who cannot play. But their problem is that they *cannot* play, not that they think it is wrong to do so. They do not fight against that which brings joy and laughter to the lives of children and adults. They yearn for it but are denied it. Almost any poor village in Africa that is not devastated by war, famine, or disease echoes with songs and laughter and games. In fact the joy of such people puts most prosperous westerners to shame.

Play even has advantages that we do not seek while playing but gain anyway. Play can renew us in body and mind. It can make us fit and healthy. It can bond us with others as we share common experiences. Children learn skills through play. It can do other good (or bad) things as well.

LEARNING TO SWIM WITH THE SHARKS

We slid into the shark cage off the southern coast of Africa. My first impression of the great white sharks circling around us was that they were very ugly, very large, and very deadly. At times, we were told, they will even come leaping out of the water to try and grab passengers off the deck.

As I stared at them through my mask, carefully keeping arms, legs, fingers, and toes at a healthy distance from the cage bars, I knew that great whites are everything Jaws *reported them to be: at that moment, they were trying to get into the cage to kill us.*

"No way I'm getting out of the cage with these *babies," I counseled myself. "Only an idiot would do that." (Some do, by the way: the world is full of idiots.)*

On other shark dives in California waters off Catalina Island, the blue, mako, and leopard sharks had been far less threatening (although they're listed as dangerous). People swim with them daily, cage or no cage. At one point, we had hung onto ropes trailing beneath the boat, in 1,500 feet of water, feeling very much like lunch (theirs, not ours). On another occasion, in a Catalina bay, we had snorkeled in six feet of water with a hundred leopard sharks cruising about us (and ignoring us).

"Why do we do this stuff?" I asked myself. "It's crazy!"

Perhaps that's why we do it. We do it for no reason, except for the sheer joy of doing it. It is a form of play, which, apart from a few side benefits, we thoroughly enjoy just for itself.

For me, apart from its sheer playfulness, shark diving has become a type of training—training for danger. It really is a little easier to deal with Chinese security police or Sudanese guerillas or Washington policy spats if you've actually played around real sharks. A "shark" lawyer is a pussycat compared to a real great white. If you can take a photograph down the throat of a twelve-foot great white at a range of two feet, knowing that it is hoping and trying to kill you, then other tight situations don't seem quite as threatening. You have less to prove, especially to yourself. The same elements exist in the exploits of climbers, skydivers, ball players, chess players, and bungee jumpers.

A brief article in the Economist *was headlined "Britain's Oldest Bungee-Jumper?" It told of seventy-eight-year-old Betty Wilson, a great-grandmother, who bungee-jumped 165 feet from a crane. When asked whether it was difficult to bungee-jump at her age, she replied, "I think it's probably easier for me than for other people. Since I'm blind, [I] can't see how far [I] fall."* [1]

Yes, there are other reasons to do crazy things. But they're only "other reasons." They're not generally the basic reason or the real reason. The real reason is simply that it's fun. It's wild. Let's do it again!

Does this sound childish and un-Christian and wasteful and useless? Certainly some forms of play can be expensive, and we have to count the cost. But in themselves, they are marvelous, right, and even godly pursuits. Why are they godly? Because they're useless, and play really is intended to be useless.

What does it mean that something is useless? We can best answer that by asking what it means to be useful. To be useful is to be good for something else, for achieveing something. A useful thing or act or practice has its goal *outside of itself.*

If we work to earn money, then we are not working for the sake of working. We do it for something else. We need money to supply our own needs and our family's needs, to help support our church, and to come to the aid of our neighbors. We work to provide service to others: we repair their cars, or build their houses, or we teach them, or we defend them in court. Working is a great thing. We need to do it, and when we can we should enjoy it. But work is not done only for its own sake. It is done for something else, for something beyond itself.

People who jog or lift weights in order to get fit or healthy or to give their body great shape are not playing. They're "working out," often more strenuously than they work at their jobs. It's not play: it's not being done for itself. It's being done for some other reason. But real play is not done for any other reason.

ONE PLAYFUL EVENING

There are few more depressing places than the lounge of an interstate Holiday Inn on a Friday night. On weeknights the businessmen are still around, and they come in and give some life to the place. But on Friday, those that can have managed to get home. And, since the hotel is on the interstate, and far from anywhere, there aren't very many locals to take the businessmen's place.

That night was like a scene from a Billy Joel song. A few scattered, leftover men were attempting to drown their sorrows while a rock band tried to generate some enthusiasm. All were unsuccessful.

About half an hour later, there was a noise at the front entrance and about sixty people in their twenties came charging in. The momentum began to pick up at once, and as the evening wore on, things got livelier. A few couples began to dance and managed to get the businessmen to join them. Soon there was improvised line dancing, which required us to move the tables.

The band caught the infectious humor and its performance level picked up several notches. Later yet, a conga line started growing, extending around the room and even out into the lobby, drawing desk clerks and waiters into its rhythm. As the line snaked back into the lounge and the music hushed for a moment, one of the band members yelled out, "This is great! Who are you guys?"

The crowd shot back, "We're evangelists!" They were, from the local College Outreach group.

Sadly, the evening ended all too soon after. We'd been in staff training down the road all week and had simply taken a break. We had to get back so we could get up early the next morning for further training and Bible study.

Did anyone become a Christian that night? Not that I know of. But nobody there will ever again think about "evangelists" in quite the same way. "Evangelists" will now mean people who are great to have around, no matter what you believe. Those young Christians were people you'd want at your party, especially if things were looking bleak, just as Jesus, according to the Gospels, seemed to be the type of person who was invited to many parties.

And, oh yes, one of the band members did become a Christian the night after.

A SOCIETY IN SEARCH OF PLAY

Just as our society never finds much rest, it also never finds much play. At first, this may sound like a strange statement; after all, we have ski resorts, amusement parks, and movie theaters galore. Play-lands are everywhere. "Play"—sometimes called "entertainment"—may be our biggest industry. But that's the point—it's an industry. It's planned, organized, earnest, strenuous, often futile, and anything but playful.

We even have what we call "professional sports." A moment's thought tells us that this is a contradiction in terms. A "sport" is, by definition, something free, spontaneous, fun, unforeseen, and open. Sport is a basic form of play. But "professional" means planned, trained, organized, and serious—a means of making a living. A real "sport" cannot be professional. A real profession cannot be sporting.

Our professional baseball, football, basketball, and hockey "players" are not "playing." It's their job, their work, their discipline. They argue over money. They claw and fight their way toward the top. The heads of the various leagues refer to "our industry" or "our product." They even go on strike (how could you go on strike from play?).

Now don't get me wrong. I love professional baseball (or at least I did until the Toronto Blue Jays went down the tubes). But while *watching* professional sports may be play, actually *participating* in pro ball is not. Play is what we do for fun, not for money. We do it for no reason except in order to do it.

There are many things we do *for* something else. This is right and good: probably most of the things we need to do are things for something else. But consider, if *everything* is for something else, where is the end point? Everything would simply be a means to something else. *But if there's nothing that is worthwhile doing in itself, then what's the point of it all?* If everything is only useful (i.e., *for something*) then what is the end point of our usefulness? What is the thing or things that everything else is for?

This is why "useless" things—things done for their own sake—are so important, so vital. *They are the ends of life.* These obviously include things far beyond play. We don't worship God for any reason other than to worship God. We don't enjoy family and friends for any reason other than to enjoy family and friends. We don't watch sunsets for any reason other than to watch sunsets. And we don't play—really, really play—except in order to do it.

This is one reason worship, faith, rest, and play are connected. Not only does rest require faith, so does play. And play is very like worship. The book of Proverbs speaks of Wisdom, personified, playing before the Lord.

> *There I was enjoying myself day after day*
> *Playing around all the time in front of God's face,*
> *Playing through the hemispheres of his earth,*
> *Having fun with all of mankind.*[2]

This mood of celebration pervades the life of Israel in the Old Testament. It shows itself in the pattern of tithes, which is something we're not inclined to relate either to play or to rejoicing. I'm sure a few pastors and church officials will be less than pleased with me for saying this, but Israel's tithes were not necessarily things that went to the temple (or now the church).

In some years tithes went to the Levites, who tended the temple. In the third year, this is what was to happen:

> *When you have finished setting aside a tenth of all your produce*
> *in the third year, the year of the tithe, you shall give it to the*

Levite, the alien (foreigner in the land), the fatherless and the widow, so that they may eat in your towns and be satisfied.

Deuteronomy 26:12, NIV
(see also Deut. 14:28–29)

According to this, the tithe went to those in need, even to foreigners. But during other years, something remarkable happened. When the place to give sacrifice was too far away, God said this:

If the road is too long for you, if you cannot bring your tithe because the place in which Yahweh chooses to make a home for his name is too far away, when Yahweh your God has blessed you, you must convert it into money and, with the money clasped in your hand, you must go to the place chosen by Yahweh your God; there you may spend the money on whatever you like, oxen, sheep, wine, fermented liquor, anything you please. There you must eat in the presence of Yahweh your God and rejoice, you and your household.

Deuteronomy 14:24–26

Let's be clear about what is happening here. If it was too far to the place of sacrifice, so that it would be hard for people bring all their goats and sheep and chickens and crops over the mountain or across the desert, they were simply to sell the animals and crops and bring the money along (it was easier to carry). Then, at the place of sacrifice, they were to buy *whatever they wanted* of food and drink, and then celebrate (and share with the Levites, v. 27). In short, God's people were to have a party, to take their tithe money and use it to eat, drink, and be merry (and share with those in need). Tithe time was party time (today's deacons try to keep this a secret)!

If I'm being flippant, I'm also being truthful. Every third year the tithes were to be consumed in a bang-up feast. Feast! That's a word that occurs a lot in the Bible, but somehow we miss out on its meaning. They had feasts—the feast of weeks, the feast of tabernacles, the feast of firstfruits.

Somehow, we don't connect the Bible word *feast* with our own word *feast*. Is this because we still think the Bible is about another "spiritual" world, not the one we live in? But on days of the Lord's feasts, Israel often ate and drank a lot, having been commanded by God to eat and drink a lot.

Not all feasts were blowouts. Some were intentionally ascetic—having no food, or else having special and sometimes bitter food (examples of these types of feasts include Passover, unleavened bread, Day of Atonement, or Yom Kippur). But the point is that some were parties. They were lively celebrations—and celebration is play. Israel's life was not one long, boring time of thrift, never consuming more than just enough. It was a rhythm—just like the rhythm of work and rest. For most of its life Israel was to be careful and frugal. The Israelites were to share with the poor and needy, and to forgive debts.

They were not wastrels who believed that they could blow whatever they wanted whenever they liked. But they also feasted. According to God's will, they took a tenth of what they had and celebrated, sometimes for a week at a time. It wasn't all play, it wasn't all rest, and it wasn't all work. But it was each of these, each done before the face of God, in obedience to God, and with thanks to God.

The first week we wandered the streets of Thessalonika, the beautiful city of Northern Greece. Phaedon ran Greece's largest private drug treatment program, and so he knew cabinet ministers and other leaders of the country. But to keep in touch with the center's staff and with what was going on, he also spent one day a week on the streets, and so he knew the druggies and prostitutes and transvestites.

Phaedon was also one of Greece's better-known singers. Consequently, when we wandered around Thessalonika's streets and squares and alleys, it was always, "Hi, Phaedon! How's it going?" from people in suits, people in leather, and people in gutters.

At midnight, the town was throbbing with life. Greeks, being more free-spirited than Americans, often don't start dinner until 11:00 P.M. (and therefore they snooze in the afternoon). We met people, and talked, and argued, and listened, and laughed, and cried. In the truest sense of the word, we lived.

A week later, we stood on the edge of the Aegean Sea, where we awaited the boat to Mt. Athos. Athos is the largest center of monasticism in Christendom. A lovely peninsula reaching out into the ocean, it is almost a self-governing country. Its population is comprised only of monks—thousands of monks. No women or even female animals are allowed to set foot on its sacred soil.

At the far end of the peninsula is the mountain itself, rising thousands of feet over the sea. Within its sheer cliffs are caves, many inhabited by hermits who have not met, seen, or spoken to anyone in years. These men devote themselves entirely to worshiping God; some do not even have a source of food.

As we waited for the boat, I said to Phaedon, "This is strange. Last week, the streets of Thessalonika, bursting with pain and hopelessness, life and joy. This week, Mt. Athos—worship beginning at 3 A.M. and carrying on all day, silent monks, simple bunk beds. It's quite a switch."

Phaedon smiled, answering as I prepared to board. "You're thinking like an Englishman—steady, level, careful, and . . . boring. Do we have to do the same thing each day, each week? Are we always supposed to be on the same level of existence? NO! That's the wrong view of moderation!

"We Greeks are moderate, too. Last week we celebrated. This week you go to the monks who fast and study. The pattern is moderate. Don't try to stay at the same level all the time. Go up and down, work and rest, party and pray. Then your life is balanced. Don't be an Englishman in a shell, who thinks he's balanced because there's nothing in his life that needs balancing because it's all flat!"

And so I set out over the blue Aegean. Behind me the taverns, the restaurants, the raucous streets, the haunting bazouki music faded away. Ahead of me was the sacred mountain, ancient, strange, silent, and mysterious. As I reflected on Phaedon's words, I concluded that I rather liked the Greek view of moderation in work and play. For that matter, I think God does, too.

OUR TASKS
IN THE WORLD

PART IV

nine

THE NATURAL WORLD

Milton was an American cocker spaniel. Tan and full of exuberance, he would bounce around, sniffing everything in sight and trying to befriend everyone and everything passing by. Milton made friends with passing people, passing dogs, passing cars, and passing boats. Though with less success, he tried to make friends with passing skunks and passing porcupines. He was about as perfect as you could get. He did, of course, have at least one problem: bad breath. On some days, one passing whiff could turn your stomach. But dogs have bad breath—it goes with the territory, so I never thought about it much.

One day, I took him in for his checkup with the vet with whom, of course, Milton tried to make friends. In between getting licked on the hands, in the ears, and on the nose, the vet managed to examine Milton. As part of the final check, he held Milton's mouth open and looked at his teeth and gums. He frowned and said, "His teeth need cleaning."

Slightly amused, I responded, "Yes, I know. I tell him that all the time, but he ignores me. I think he has a problem holding the brush between his paws."

The vet shook his head. "No, I'm serious. His teeth have got to be brushed."

I said, "You mean I have to brush my dog's teeth?"

"Yes, you."

"But that's crazy. Dogs have managed to survive in the wild for thousands of years without brushing their teeth. Wild dogs, wolves, and dingoes still seem to live quite well without visits from dental hygienists. This is absurd."

The vet explained patiently (he'd obviously done this before), "Yes, but wolves don't usually get into the garbage or steal candy when you're not looking. They don't have sugar cravings. But more to the point, dogs in the wild never live long enough to have to worry about their teeth. They die long before rotten teeth could even become a problem. It's only domestic dogs that are going to live ten or twelve or fourteen years. They are healthy enough that we have to worry about their teeth."

It had never really hit me before that wild animals don't have it better than domestic ones. Of course I know that most pets are perpetually pampered. But I'd somehow assumed that wild animals were always fitter, leaner, tougher, healthier. They're not. Usually they live in a scramble for survival. They typically die painfully and often young. Animals are not always better when left alone, freed from the supposedly polluting touch of human beings.

The natural world is not some self-contained universe of harmonious bliss, which would survive in pristine magnificence without the presence of people. Nature is not independent; it is one part of God's good creation, and it is created in relation to human beings. It is made, in part, for us, just as we are made, in part, for it. As human beings, we are responsible not only for our social world but also for the natural world itself.

GOD'S VIEW OF NATURE

Nature is important to God and, therefore, important to us. It is not a passing fancy destined for final destruction. Nor is it divine, as though it should not be touched or altered. We are called neither to exploit it according to our own desires, nor to deify it as some pristine idol. Both it and we will only flourish when we take up our responsibility for nature as its faithful stewards.

In earlier chapters, I have emphasized that when we think of creation, we shouldn't think only of the natural world: creation includes schools, homes, churches, and planes as much as oceans, forests, flowers, and deer. But the natural world is a major part of creation. God made it all and said that it was good, and even now he continues to care for it day by day.

God did not just make the world and then leave it alone to run like clockwork. He steadfastly loves and provides for his creatures. The psalmist cried out to God in wonder:

> *You make springs break out in the gullies,*
> *so that their waters run between the hills.*
> *The wild beasts all drink from them,*
> *the wild asses quench their thirst;*
> *the birds of the air nest on their banks*
> *and sing among the leaves.*

From your high pavilion you water the hills;
the earth is enriched by your provision.
You make grass grow for the cattle
and green things for those who toil for people,
bringing bread out of the earth
and wine to gladden human hearts,
oil to make their faces shine
and bread to sustain their strength.
The trees of the Lord are green and leafy,
the cedars of Lebanon which God has planted;
the birds build their nests in them,
the stork makes her home in their tops.
High hills are the haunt of the mountain-goat,
and boulders a refuge for the rock-badger.

You have made the moon to measure the year
and taught the sun where to set.
When you make darkness and it is night,
all the beasts of the forest come forth
the young lions roar for prey,
seeking their food from God.
When you make the sun rise, they slink away
and go to rest in their lairs;
but people come out to their work
and to their labors until evening.

Countless are the things you have made, O Lord.
You have made all by your wisdom;

and the earth is full of your creatures,
beasts great and small.

Psalm 104:10–25

God's care extends not only toward each facet of human life but to the animals and the earth itself. God gives the animals what they need: homes for storks and bears and badgers, food and drink for asses and lions. The good things in the world are gifts that God gives to sustain human beings, animals, and plants, day by day and second by second.

NOAH, THE FIRST ENVIRONMENTALIST

God loves his creation, and he covenants with it. The story of Noah brings this to light. When God decided to destroy the earth by flood, he chose to save a remnant. As we noted in chapter 3, God not only saved a remnant of *people* but also of the *animals*. As God instructed, Noah gathered two of every kind of animal that made its home on the land or in the air and made sure that he had the right types of food for them (Gen. 6:20–21). This rescue wasn't just for farm animals, to provide Noah with food; it included wild animals as well. Noah might be considered the patron saint of environmentalists.

Had Noah been a modern evangelical, he might have decided to ignore a couple of animals in order to squeeze in more people. But God said no, he wanted only some people on the vessel; the rest of the place was for animals.

Nor did God just seal up the ark and forget about its inhabitants. As the ark drifted over the water, God "remembered Noah and all the wild animals and the livestock that were with him in the ark" (Gen. 8:1).

After the ark had landed, God promised never again to destroy the earth with a flood. This covenant was made not just with Noah or the people on the ark. It was made with all the inhabitants of the ark—*with every living creature.* "I now establish my covenant with you and with your descendants after you, *and with every living creature* that was with you—the birds, the livestock and all the wild animals, all those that came out of the ark with you—every living creature on earth" (Gen. 9:9–10).

God's covenant promise with the earth is repeated over and over—in verses 12, 13, 15, 16, and 17. (See also Hos. 2:18–22.) God wants us to get the point. The rainbow is "the sign of the covenant between me *and the earth*" (v. 13 NIV).

The Bible's teaching on the natural world should keep us from two common modern errors. The first error is to treat the earth as if it belongs to us, as though we can use it however we like. Tied in with this is the idea that the earth only exists to provide things for human beings. Phil Gaglardi, the former Highways Minister in British Columbia, Canada, is reputed to have once said, "God wouldn't have put all those trees there if he didn't intend for us to cut them down."

The other error is to treat the natural world as if it were some self-contained, pristine thing that should always be left alone, never to be interfered with by human beings. The modern world has a lot of romanticism about nature and often portrays nature as perfect in itself—its only problems coming from human interference.

LETTING NATURE TAKE ITS COURSE

The difficulties with this latter view show themselves in America's national parks. The Park Service switches back and forth between the view that the parks should be adjusted to serve the desires of visitors and the view that they should be left alone in natural splendor. A hundred political pressure groups try to push them one way or another. And there is simply no way to resolve this dilemma.

One issue that demonstrates the division of opinion concerns how to deal with forest fires. Fires have existed since long before human beings spread across America. Some trees, like Sequoias, cannot reproduce without fire. Fire is "natural." But when, in 1988, eight hundred thousand acres in Yellowstone went up in smoke (over a third of the entire park), there was intense pressure to put the fires out, as had often been done before. People complained that we could not stand by and see the animals and the beauty devastated. We must interfere, we must put out the fires. We can't let nature take its course, or nature will destroy nature.

Now elk are reproducing rapidly throughout the park and threaten to destroy the vegetation. If this continues, the elk will starve. Some people want to save the elk (and the plants) by reducing their numbers through the simple expedient of shooting lots of them. Others say that winter and starvation will take care of the elk. Meanwhile, when the elk migrate out of the park, Wyoming feeds them—so the elk can go back in and chew up more of the grazing lands.

Are we "preserving nature" in an untouched state when we keep elk alive, or when we let them starve, or when we feed them, or when we shoot them? Should we leave nature somehow "untouched"?

There's absolutely no answer to these questions simply because there is no self-contained "nature," independent of human beings. Humanity is not "unnatural." We are as much a part of this planet as the elk are, and we live in relation to the elk. "Nature" includes us.

There is no way of doing things that will not "interfere" with Yellowstone, or with anything else in the creation. We live in the middle of it. We don't have the option to make no choices, to leave "nature" alone. We have only the option to make wise choices.

BIBLICAL ENVIRONMENTALISM

The biblical picture is neither one of careless exploitation nor one of non-interference. The key is that God has made us as the *stewards* of the earth. When God said, "Fill the earth and subdue it. Rule over . . . every living creature" (Gen. 1:28), this was not a mandate for domination. A short time later God showed Adam what it meant. "The Lord God took the man and put him in the Garden of Eden to work it and take care of it" (Gen. 2:15). The word *work* here is often translated elsewhere in the Bible as "serve," and the words *take care of* are often translated "keep." For example, when Aaron blessed the Israelites, he said, "The LORD bless you and keep you" (Num. 6:24). We are to take care of the earth in the way that God takes care of us.

There are always two aspects of God's command to us as stewards. The two senses are to properly cultivate the earth *and* to preserve it, to use it and maintain it.

The world is entrusted to us by a God who loves it and wants us to care for it. He entrusted it to *us*. We humans have a genuine authority over the plants and animals; we are not simply to be dissolved into an ecological flux wherein we touch nothing. But our authority is the authority of the steward, the caretaker. When Joel looks ahead in his famous prophecy of those days when . . .

> *I will pour out my Spirit on all people. Your sons and daughters will prophesy, your old men will dream dreams, your young men will see visions. Even on my servants, both men and women, I will pour out my Spirit in those days.*
>
> Joel 2:28–29

. . . he ties it firmly together with hope for the animals as well: "Be not afraid, O wild animals, for the open pastures are becoming green. The trees are bearing their fruit; the fig tree and the vine yield their riches" (v. 22). The Spirit-filled people are also a promise to the animals.

Environmental problems are not caused by genuine human stewardship but by greed and sin. Hosea and Isaiah both depict this:

> *Hear the word of the LORD, you Israelites,*
> *because the LORD has a charge to bring against you who live*
>   *in the land:*
> *"There is no faithfulness, no love, no acknowledgment of God*
>   *in the land.*
> *There is only cursing, lying and murder, stealing and adultery;*
> *they break all bounds, and bloodshed follows bloodshed.*

Because of this the land mourns,
and all who live in it waste away;
the beasts of the field and the birds of the air
and the fish of the sea are dying."

Hosea 4:1–3

The earth dries up and withers,
the world languishes and withers, the exalted of the earth languish.
The earth is defiled by its people;
they have disobeyed the laws, violated the statutes
and broken the everlasting covenant.

Isaiah 24:4–5

When there is no faithfulness and love, the beasts and the birds die. When there is disobedience, the world withers. Instead of environmental greed or environmental romanticism, we need environmental stewardship. What does this mean? Stewardship is an extremely broad term. A steward is someone who is appointed by the owner of property to manage the affairs of the household. Historically, the typical steward made sure that the servants were well looked after or at least were obedient (only wealthy households could have stewards). He also made sure that the animals were healthy, the crops were planted and harvested properly, the children were behaving, and investments were made wisely. Such stewards were common illustrations in Jesus' parables: he used them as examples, both good and bad ones, of how the disciples should behave as citizens of the kingdom of God (see Luke 12:35–48; 16:1–13; 19:11–27).

The steward was to stand in the master's stead, to look after affairs in the way the master wanted, and to give account to the master of what he had done. This is why stewardship is one way of describing the task of humankind on the earth. Humans are God's stewards, standing in God's stead. We look after his property, and we will give an account to him of what we have done with it.

CHRISTIAN "DOMINATION" OF NATURE?

In recent times the Christian faith has been severely criticized for supposedly advocating the domination of nature because of the teaching to "fill and subdue" the earth. But this concept is miles apart from the biblical teaching of tending and caring for creation. Perhaps we could agree that what the Bible says is one thing but that what we Christians have actually taught and done is entirely another matter. After all, Christians have often violated biblical teaching in lots of other things. Yet, even in terms of Christians' actual conduct, this critique of the Christian faith is wide of the mark.

The theme of the domination of nature only became a strong theme in the seventeenth century. The increasing exploitation of nature since the eighteenth century coincides with the decline of Christianity as a formative force in the West. Rather than looking for the spiritual roots of our present exploitation in the Christian faith, we might better look to the humanist creed, "Man is the measure of all things," which has produced the greatest disjuncture between the human world and the natural world.

If man is the only measure, then nature can only exist *for* man and can have no value of its own, hence it can be exploited with impunity. But the Bible does not teach either that "man is the measure" or the equally false modern idea that "nature is the measure of all things." Rather it teaches that both of these are idolatry. It is *God* alone who is the measure of all things, and he commands the proper relation between man and nature. He sets our bounds in relation to one another.

Since our task is to be stewards of the earth and all that is in it, we must have a clearer idea of what is required of us. First, we are the stewards not only of natural things like land, soil, trees, oceans, and minerals. We are the stewards of all things—including time, energy, health, organization, family life, work styles, buildings—everything that exists in human life.

Second, to steward all these things is to treat them in the way that God calls us to treat them. This means carefully attending to all the ways in which we can express love—through beauty, through preservation, and through proper use. To be a steward of something is to be aware of its proper place in God's creation, to be sensitive to the ways it can be misused, to recognize the ways it can bring benefits to others, and to preserve it and cause it to be "fruitful"—caring for it so that what is good is conserved and using it so that it brings blessing.

The word in the New Testament that we translate as "stewardship" is *oikonomia*, the management of the household, the *oikos*. It is from these words that we get our word *economics*: true economics should be understood as a form of stewardship. It means using things wisely, carefully, and efficiently. And it means considering what happens to the natural world as well when we make decisions, whether as individuals or families or corporations.

It is not my goal here to try to outline what this might mean in practical or concrete terms. I am only striving, here as elsewhere, to outline the spiritual principles that are at stake in how we treat the world that God has placed in our hands. We are looking after the world that God made through Jesus Christ. When Jesus returns we will need to give an account of our stewardship. As he said to Peter: "Who, then, is the wise and trustworthy steward whom the master will place over his household to give them at their proper time their allowance of food? Blessed is that servant if his master's arrival finds him doing exactly that" (Luke 12:42–43, NJB).

The sun slowly came up, and as we walked over the snow it stopped making the squealing sound it makes at about minus 15° and started making that crunching noise that it makes at about minus 5°. The sky was a crystalline, piercing blue, and the snow lay heavy on the trees roundabout. The smoke from the fire rose in a straight, unwavering column. The air, almost unnaturally still, contrasted starkly and strangely with the bustle of over a hundred dogs who were staring, leaping, snuffling, and barking as we carried their harnesses toward the sleds.

We were off for our first day of dogsledding. And our boisterous excitement was more than matched by the dogs themselves. Our first task was to set up the harnesses and then to fetch the dogs—six of them for each sled—that were going to do the pulling. We had a tough day ahead of us, and the chosen dogs would have a tougher one. We had to cover about 35 miles to our campsite before nightfall, and the days were short.

I was told which dogs I should collect. First the wheel dogs, the larger dogs who would be right in front of the sled, taking most of the strain. Then the lead dog, who was a mutt and not very big, but she was smart and knew how to take the lead.

As I went out to get the first dog, all the animals in front of me leaped up and down, barking and straining at their tethers. They weren't trying to get away from me; they were trying to get my attention. They wanted to go along. It was as if a hundred voices were saying, "Take me! Take me! I'll go! I'll go!" As I'd pass by a dog, en route to one beyond, it would lie down again in the snow with sad eyes and drooping tail. "Maybe not today," it seemed to sigh.

The dogs weren't always kind about it, either. When we'd bring one dog back through the pack, the others would bark, growl, and nip at it. The air was filled with yelps of resentment, "Why him? What's he got that I don't have? I'm a better dog than he is any day of the week."

The same drama would replay each time we went back to get another dog. There was renewed hope among the animals, only to be dashed again for most of them.

When we finally got the six dogs in harness, their barking started anew as we tried to get ourselves and our equipment ready. The dogs were increasingly frustrated. "What's the hold up? What's going on back there? Let's move! Let's go!" We had to make sure the sled was firmly tied to a strong post, otherwise the dogs would have gladly set out on their own. They kept trying to do it anyway.

The first rule of amateur dogsledding is this: Never let go of the sled. This rule is essential because, unless you stop them, the dogs are going to go. And unless you have hold of the sled, they are *going to go without you. An expert knows how to get them back. But for the rest of us, it would simply mean watching our sled, and all our gear and supplies, disappear down the trail and over the hill. This is not a cheerful prospect with the thermometer dropping toward minus 30°, with night coming on and a ten-hour walk home.*

As for the dogs, they'd just keep going a hundred miles without us if they could. They wouldn't even look back. For them it would be that much more fun without the human cargo. "The sled seems lighter now, doesn't it?"

After we arrived at our campsite, we fed the dogs and then ourselves. We crawled into the tent and collapsed into our sleeping bags. Outside, a few minutes later, one dog howled, then another took it up, and then all of them formed a chorus. They howled together for thirty or forty seconds, the sound echoing through the still woods. And then, just as quickly, they stopped, lay down, and went to sleep. They did this every night.

Some people claim that dogsledding is cruel, and no doubt with some people there may be cruelty. But what I cannot accept for one instant is the idea that simply sledding with dogs misuses or mistreats them. For these dogs, dinner was the only thing to be greeted with more anticipation than a day on the trail. There was nothing they wanted more than to go with us.

ten

Our Political Responsibility

On the English TV program I was watching, a group of civil liber-tarians defended an almost absolute right to publish freely. They were aghast at any suggestion that there should not be a paperback version of Salman Rushdie's The Satanic Verses. *Even though there was a death warrant against the author from the Iranian government, and even though the book obviously pained many Muslims deeply, these libertarians thought that there could never be a reason to censor free expression. They demanded that the gov-ernment remove any barriers to the paperback's free publication and wide circulation. They said this was their political position.*

The second segment of the show involved relatives and friends of hostages being held in Lebanon. They felt that the government was not doing enough to secure the hostages' release—too afraid of losing face and of giving up too much. Why had the French been able to make much better headway with their hostages? The relatives felt that the government should not stand on pride or abstract principle but should be willing to negotiate to obtain the captives' release. They called this their political position.

The producer had a rare brain wave or perhaps an insight into what is really involved in politics. The third segment of the show brought the two groups—the civil libertarians and the hostage supporters—together in the same discussion.

The interviewer then asked the hard question (i.e., the real polit-ical question): "If the terms for the release of some hostages was the suppression of The Satanic Verses, *would you do it?" (This was not a far-fetched suggestion—such a demand was made.) "What if the hostages would be killed if the book were not withdrawn?"*

This question produced a rare moment of silence for a televi-sion panel. The civil libertarians hemmed and hawed. No one was willing to publicly accept the death of a known person in order to defend his or her principles (especially if that someone's wife were sitting opposite).

The relatives and friends were more forthright. "Absolutely yes!" they said. "If that's a condition, meet it. Withdraw the book—free real flesh-and-blood human beings, not printed pages."

The discussion continued, but in a wayward fashion. The diamond-hard moment had come and gone. Briefly, the question had been no longer a "political demand" but a real life question, a genuine political question. It was no longer a debate about one single ideal, one single demand, or one single good. Now there were many ideals, many goods, many demands taken together. And these different demands of different people were not all achievable at the same time.

CHRISTIANS AND POLITICS

In his *Screwtape Letters*, C. S. Lewis remarks that Christians make two equal and opposite mistakes about evil spirits. One mistake is to treat belief in them as a superstitious relic, a hangover from a previous benighted age. The other mistake is to become obsessed with them, treating them as the underlying cause of everything.

Lewis was right about our view of evil spirits. A similar thing occurs when evangelicals try to come to terms with politics. For some, politics is the work of the devil. It is simply evil, manipulative, self-centered, power hungry: the very epitome of what the Bible condemns as "worldly."

For others, politics has become an important part of our Christian life, especially since the United States seems to be increasingly overtaken by distinctively non-Christian and immoral beliefs, practices, and laws. But instead of soberly appreciating the true importance of politics, the issue has become an obsession, as though politics alone holds the key to the future. When this happens, emotions run amuck and hearts and hopes soar and plummet with each election.

Politics certainly has its share of problems. As someone once said, "You have to be crazy to go into politics, and the crazier you are, the further you get." Ambrose Bierce, in his wickedly funny *The Devil's Dictionary*, defines politics as "*n.* A strife of interests masquerading as a contest of principles. The conduct of public affairs for private advantage." This is partly true, but it is equally certainly only *part* of the truth. The problems, frustrations, egomania, and hypocrisy of politics are not the slightest bit unusual in *any* area of human life.

Politics is most assuredly rife with sin, but this is merely a simple reflection of the fact that human beings in general are rife with sin. Exactly the same power plays and conflicts we encounter in politics also occur in our offices, our factories, our schools and, let us be honest, in our families and our churches.

In actual fact, I've seen more bitter conflicts in churches than I have in the political arena.

No matter what our personal reaction may be, politics, the art of governing large numbers of people in a country, is not optional. One way or another, people *will* be governed. It is only part, but it is an important part, of our God-given responsibility. It is yet another divine service. We cannot escape it, nor should we want to.

POLITICS: IN THE BEGINNING

The first biblical appearance of what we can call politics comes in the fourth chapter of Genesis. Cain, in a fit of jealousy, murders his brother Abel. God, who is just, appears and challenges Cain, asking, "Where is your brother?" Cain tries to put God off with the dismissive words, "Am I my brother's keeper?" (Gen. 4:8–9).

Sometimes we treat these words as if they were somehow genuine Christian teaching, as if we really were *not* responsible for our brothers and sisters. We must remember that these are the words spoken by the first murderer when faced with his crime. We *are* our brothers' keepers. We are deeply responsible before God for what happens to others. This responsibility has many facets, and politics is only one. But it is an indispensable one.

When God appeared to Cain, he appeared as a judge. He said that Abel's blood "cried out," appealing to the Lord, calling for him to render judgment. God appears therefore as a righteous judge, administering punishment for Cain's crime. The word translated here as "cries out" occurs many times in the Bible. Sometimes it means simply the cry of an animal. At other times it is a call for God's help and justice. The poor and needy "cried out" for the destruction of Sodom and Gomorrah (see Gen. 18:20; Ezek. 16:49). When the Israelites were slaves in Egypt, they "cried out" for God to rescue them (Exod. 2:23, 24). Perhaps the best English translation for "cries out" is "appeal." It can be a simple cry of pain, or an appeal for help, or a direct legal appeal for justice.

Abel's blood appealed to God for justice. God's just punishment was exile, and Cain was driven off to a far land. But even then God did not forget him; he provided Cain with a sign, a mark that was intended to protect him. The "mark of Cain" was a sign of God's protection so that those who tried to exact further punishment upon Cain—more than what God himself had already decreed and administered—would themselves face punishment.[1]

With this first crime it was God himself who did the judging. But since he had appointed humankind as the stewards of the earth to exercise responsibility over the entire creation, God also decided to transfer responsibility to human beings themselves to deal with injustice in their midst. This is vividly portrayed in the story of Noah. With Cain, it was God who had been the judge. After the flood, God said to those who came out of the ark, "Whoever sheds the blood of man *by man* shall his blood be shed; for in the image of God has God made man" (Gen. 9:6, emphasis added).

Here God stresses the *importance* of human life because we are made in the image of God. Killing human beings demands a penalty. But God equally stresses the *responsibilities* of human life, also because we are made in the image of God. Because human beings have authority and responsibility, *it is we who now have to exact that penalty*. Whereas, with Cain, it was God who acted directly, with Noah and his descendants—which include us—it is human beings who have the responsibility to act. To this day, we are the ones called by God to execute his justice upon the earth.

This is why God educated and trained Abraham in doing justice. When God was contemplating the fate of Sodom and Gomorrah, he said to himself, "Shall I hide from Abraham what I am about to do? Abraham will surely become a great and powerful nation and all nations on earth will be blessed through him. For I have chosen him, so that he will direct his children and his household after him to keep the way of the Lord by doing what is right and just"(Gen. 18:17–19).

God seemed to use this occasion as an apprenticeship for Abraham so that he would learn what it means to be a just judge. Abraham took up his responsibility and then argued with God as to whether the cities should be destroyed. "What if there are fifty righteous people?" Abraham asked. Would it be just to kill these righteous people along with the unrighteous? In the end God agreed with Abraham that if there were even ten righteous people, he would not destroy the city (see Gen. 18:23–33). Abraham had become a judge, working out the proper requirements of justice.

Through Noah and Abraham has come our responsibility to deal with justice and injustice in human affairs. This pattern continued through Moses, who gave the law to Israel. Moses did not create the law; that was already given by God. But Moses had to judge individual cases before the law. No law itself determines the outcome of a case; it needs a judge to carry the law's intent out. When this job became too strenuous for him, Moses, on the advice of his father-in-law, appointed additional judges to handle the less important cases (see Exod. 18:13–26).

CALLED TO JUDGE, CALLED TO RULE

Throughout the history of Israel, the Bible carefully records the judicial and political structures that develop in the books of Judges, Samuel, and Kings. The judges in Israel were to decide what constituted good and evil in Israel's life. Later on came the appearance of kings and, combined with them, of prophets, whose job it was to challenge the kings in terms of God's law. In fact, the Bible gives far more attention to what judges and kings do than it does to the activities of the priests of the tabernacle or the temple. The people we most remember in the Bible are those like Joshua, a military leader, or Daniel, a royal counselor, or David and Solomon, Israel's great kings. These were deeply spiritual men, but they were not priests, nor did they serve in the temple. They had political roles.

The responsibility of political leadership is divinely given, but it is quite different from the role of priests. In the Bible, the two roles become clearly distinct. In fact, two kings, Jereboam and Uzziah, were severely punished (one by death from leprosy) for taking over the role of the priests and offering sacrifices, even though their motives were not bad ones (see 1 Kings 12:25–13:6; 2 Chron. 26:16ff). (In this sense, "separation of church and state" is not an American invention but has roots in the Old Testament.)

This theme does not disappear in the New Testament. While the life of the church has many differences from the life of the nation of Israel, God is still concerned with the political structures under which we live. When the Apostle Paul addresses this in his letter to the Romans, he emphasizes that the governing powers are "God's servants" who are appointed "to do you good" (Rom. 13:4). Jesus said that "all power in heaven and earth" was given to him (Matt. 28:18). When Paul proclaimed that Jesus creates, upholds, and redeems every aspect of the world, he emphasized that this included even political things—"thrones, dominions, principalities and powers" (Col. 1:16). As far as the Word of God is concerned, politics is not something separate and apart from service to Jesus Christ.

In our own day, we should not imagine that God is only concerned with what goes on inside our churches, with what pastors or elders or deacons do. God is intimately and directly concerned with what laws are given to the whole society and how these laws are carried out. Politics is one of God's basic concerns.

POLITICAL AUTHORITY AND CHRISTIANITY

A Christian understanding of politics requires real human judgment and responsibility. It is not simply a case of taking some Old Testament law or New Testament principle and setting it down to be enforced in the middle of our own very different situation. There is no one type of political order commended in the Scriptures. However, there are consistent guidelines for what all political authorities are to be and to do as servants of God.[2] Political authority is always related to *justice*—protecting everyone's rightful place in God's world (see Ps. 45:4–8; 72:1–4). The apostles express this as rightly rewarding good and judiciously condemning evil (Rom. 13:1–8; 1 Pet. 2:13, 14). A major part of doing justice is defending the poor, the widow and the orphan, and others who need protection (see Exod. 22:21–24; Deut. 10:7, 18; Ps. 72).

The Scriptures also stress that government should be *impartial.* Judges are to be like God, not least in the sense that they are not to be respecters of persons: they must treat all alike. God declared his love for the foreigner and the sojourner in Israel and called judges to be impartial in conflicts between Israelites and strangers (see Deut. 10:17–19; Exod. 23:12; Jer. 23:3). He calls for equality before the law. This shows that the people of God should not expect any undue favors from a godly ruler if they are in the wrong. A Christian ruler should give no special privilege to Christians.

Political rulers are also *limited.* They should not try to claim the total or the final allegiance of human beings, otherwise they have ceased being servants and are trying to take over God's place and authority. While Paul affirms that the powers that be are God's servants (Rom. 13:1–8), Peter also tells us that "we must obey God rather than men" (Acts 5:29, see also 4:19 and 1 Pet. 2:13–14). These are combined in Jesus' admonition to give to God the things that are God's and to Caesar the things that are Caesar's (Mark 12: 13–17). Neither a president, nor a legislature, nor a court, nor a constitution, nor a people (or bishop or boss or pastor or parent) can claim to be the total or final authority. God has many types of servants, and they have different authorities. Government is neither the final nor the central authority in human life: it must know its God-given limits. One of these limits is what we now call "democracy."

THE OLD TESTAMENT CASE FOR DEMOCRACY

The Bible does not directly advocate "democracy" or, indeed, any other specific form of government. Nevertheless there are grounds for believing that "democracy" (government that is representative of the people) reflects God's will for political arrangements. Monarchy entered Israel's life only reluctantly and with dire warning from God about its negative consequences (1 Sam. 8:11–18). After the Exodus, the Israelites saw themselves as God's free slaves, subject to him alone (see Judg. 8:23). The Bible is consistent in viewing any form of authority as a form of servanthood (Matt. 20:8; Mark 9:25). Elders (variously described as "princes," "foremen," "heads," and "leaders"; (see Exod. 5:6; 15:19; 19:7; Num. 1:16; 11:16; 26:9) derived their authority from God and were often appointed by such people as Moses or Samuel. But at the same time they are also described as being *chosen* by the people of Israel (see Deut. 19; Num. 1:16; 11:16; 26:9).

The people of Israel were called to consent to the laws and to commit themselves to God's commands (Exod. 3:16ff; 19:7ff). When Saul was chosen king by God, he was also elected from among the people by lot (1 Sam. 8–10). The people shared in the responsibility of political office by helping to choose their leaders and committing themselves to honor and obey them.

Israel's political life was marked by covenants among kings, the elders, the people, and God, wherein Israel took on a corporate and collective responsibility to uphold the law of God (2 Sam. 5:3; Deut. 27). Hence leaders and people were responsible to one another and mutually responsible to God. Political authority is not a "theocracy" but an act of self-government and responsibility. This is the root of a biblical notion of democracy.[3]

THE CHALLENGES OF DEMOCRACY

In a democratic form of politics, however, there are many difficulties with which we must contend. First, if governments are responsible to their *entire population*, we as Christians have to respect and *give room to others* in the society to exercise their responsibility, whether they are Christian or not.

Second, at the same time, *governments cannot always simply do what most of the people want.* Since all people are sinful, the majority of the population could well desire something that is fundamentally unjust. It's not just dictatorships that do evil. Even elected governments, like that of Nazi Germany, can do hideous injustice.

Third, if they are to be genuinely democratic, *governments cannot simply ignore what the people want.* A biblical view of politics requires governments *both* to be responsible and to do justice as well as be responsible to the population at large in deciding what justice is. Therefore politics involves the need to do what is right *and* the responsibility to win popular support for what is right. If one of these is lacking, we will degenerate into either pragmatism or authoritarianism.

A Christian view of politics necessarily has these "democratic" elements, but as we well know "the people" are usually divided in their views. In most cases, there is no simple, direct answer to what the people want. This means that we must be open to the whole messiness of what also is called "politics": the attempt to persuade people of what it is right to do and to try to gather popular support for a course of action. Since this takes place in an arena of millions of people, it requires a principled attempt to make deals, build coalitions, share power, trade off, give everyone a place, and get half a loaf rather than none. Christians are often uncomfortable with politics in this sense. It seems unprincipled—compromised— and we would much prefer some direct official implementation of a true principle.

However, messy as it is, the alternative to vote grubbing and opinion shaping is authoritarianism or totalitarianism. The chaotic nature of elections and politics is typical of how all democratic societies are run. If we take seriously the divine authority of being doers of justice, stewards of political power, and responsible to the people, we must take "politics" seriously. Often the compromising and trimming nature of politics is summarized in the true cliché that "politics is the art of the possible." A useful expansion of this was given by French President Jacques Chirac: "Politics is not the art of the possible, but the art of making possible what is necessary." Perhaps as Christians we should expand this to: "Politics is the art of gaining support and making possible that which is right." As Christians we are called to enter into this frustrating and freeing, exhausting and exhilarating struggle to make possible what is right.

MODERN-DAY CRUSADES

If we take our political responsibility seriously, one of our greatest needs is for political discernment. Most political matters cannot be reduced to a few biblical texts. Hence we always need to work with a comprehensive overview of our *whole* political task and the proper role of government. We also need to be careful about the *manner* of our politics. Too often, Christian political efforts are imagined and described as "crusades."

"Crusades" have several drawbacks. One is that they suffuse politics with military and warlike metaphor. Since there are very real wars in the world, sometimes this might be necessary. But more often, in day-to-day affairs, it merely poisons the atmosphere, demonizes opponents, and does greater harm than good. A "crusade" also implies a campaign with a single end, and one soon to be achieved. This ends up reducing politics to an "issue" or a set of "issues" instead of the ongoing and never-ending task of running the public life of a people. Furthermore, it drains energy in a short-term effort so that when the "crusade" is finished, whether in success or failure, the effort, and often much future effort, is abandoned.

As Jim Skillen has pointed out: "Politics is not something done in a moment of passion with a simple moral zealousness. Politics is more like raising a family, or running a business, or stewarding a farm. It requires lifelong commitment, patience, steadiness, and great attention to detail day after day."

POLITICS, RIGHTS, AND RESTORATION

Like many Americans, both Christian and non-Christian, I sometimes get fed up with peoples' incessant demands for their "rights." Rights for this, rights for that. We hear astounding claims that every problem we face is somehow someone else's fault, that every difficulty means that we are entitled to something. But when we see people who really *do* lack basic human rights, we realize why human rights are so important in the modern world.

Politics is not simply a fight about who gets what. It is not merely a realm of struggle and sin. It is also a ministry, protecting the lives of human beings, God's image bearers. It is a means of bringing justice and dignity. The restoration of decent politics is a Christian ministry. It is a hard and necessary ministry, and we need to take it up.

A hot, steaming day found us traveling down to the coast with a friend, a high-ranking Malaysian judge who was both Christian and ethnic Chinese. A Christian group was running training sessions for Christian leaders from among the Orang Asli, *the indigenous tribal peoples of Malaysia.*

Malaysian tribal peoples suffer from the widespread discrimination and harassment that afflicts many tribal peoples throughout the world. They are at the bottom rung of the social ladder, regarded as primitive and stupid, and frequently at risk of losing their land and their homes. These particular people, many of whom live in the wild and inhospitable jungles of Borneo, are Christian believers. This compounds their difficulties: they suffer not only because of their status as tribal peoples but also because they are Christians in a predominately Muslim country.

Many told stories about being stopped, questioned, unfairly arrested, hassled, and occasionally beaten by police. Most of them do not know that they have any legal protection from this treatment. The judge had come to help them understand their legal rights.

This was not the first time the judge had led one of these workshops. And in the discussion period following his talk, some members of the group told of their experiences in the months following his previous presentation. One man in particular, an elder in the church, recounted his encounter with the authorities.

One night he had been walking along the road, returning to his home. The police had stopped him and questioned him about what he was doing. He answered them politely and openly—he saw no reason not to cooperate with policemen who were simply doing their jobs. But as time went on, they became more aggres-

sive, more contemptuous. The man recalled what he had been taught by the judge. Politely but firmly he said, "Well, it was nice talking to you, but time's getting on, and I have to be about my business. If you have no charges or complaints against me, then I have a right to freely go on my way, and you have no right whatever to detain me." For good measure, he even quoted part of the legal code. The police immediately let him go on.

The tribesman told this story with a sense of awe, of wonder. The words had seemed to him almost like some spiritual incantation. He'd been advised, "Say this to the police and they will let you go." To his amazement, they had done just that. He had touched on the fact that he had rights: that God has said that he must be respected and that this had been made into law. He had touched on the God-given purposes of political power.

eleven

I MAGINATION
AND THE ARTS

The photographs in the church basement displayed alongside paintings and sculpture and glasswork and weaving shone with a burst of color. To a professional eye, there were certainly many more accomplished photographs around. But for the amateur passerby, the riotous colors of the exhibition seemed to have a powerful attraction.

Against an evening sky of burnt orange and brown, flickering color carelessly laid across the lazy ocean waves, a silhouetted villager on Timor launched his boat.

The majestic splendor of the Grand Canyon was dappled with cloud and shadow, with a retreating storm leaving behind a rainbow as a parting gift.

The lighthouse at Peggy's Cove appeared starkly in razor-cut white and red, standing almost too solid, too substantial to be real against a rare blue cloudless Maritime sky.

The roofs of the Imperial Palace in Seoul, Korea, with criss-crossing arches and eaves painted in multihued patterns, left the eye confused until the image took shape.

The cherry blossoms in Kyoto, each leaf carved, each stem winding with crooked artistry, seemed to vibrate with life against a stark black wall.

As I looked at the photographs, I still wondered where they'd originated. Part of me knew the answer very well. I had, after all, taken the photographs. Another part of me couldn't account for the fact that they had something to do with me. I have always taken photographs and, having been fortunate enough to travel, could take photographs of wild and wonderful things.

Occasionally I'd show them to people, who had admired them. But, in recent years, more people had said, "You should show these." I was reluctant to do so, since these pictures had required little skill, little effort, and very little thought. They had just come, almost as though they had taken themselves. If people asked me how to take photographs, I would answer truthfully, not sarcastically, "Well, you point the camera at something, and if looks good, you press the button."

To me, it seemed extravagant to think of my photographs as some form of "art," but there they were, in an exhibition of artworks. And people were enjoying them.

To be able to see things, picture things, imagine things, create things, and envision possibilities is just as important to the world as the gifts of laboring and reasoning. Without these gifts, much of our world would be cold and gray. Our books would be flat, didactic prose. Our buildings would be awkward, functional lumps. Our homes would be barracks with only necessary things placed in the most useful and easiest way. Our worship would be mere rote. Our lives would be mere function.

But God made us more than functional creatures: He made us imaginative and artistic creatures. This, too, is part of the image of God, since God himself is an artist.

THE MASTER ARTIST

After the flood, God gave a sign of his promise that never again would the world be destroyed by water. He didn't just record the covenant on parchment. He did not set it down in basic black and white. Instead, God's sign and seal of promise was a rainbow, a splendor set in the heavens (see Gen. 9:13). It was a sign of shimmering, colorful light containing within itself the promise the world would be preserved, and preserved as a place of richness and beauty.

God expresses this richness not only with rainbows but also with sunsets. Even as I write this, the sky is tinting mauve and orange. Hundreds of people will gather at the California coast to watch the splendor—they do so each time the afternoon sky begins to hint of glories to come. God paints the sky every evening, and it draws more viewers than all of the galleries in all of the world. And each sunset is different: as Picasso said, "God is the greatest artist; he never does the same thing twice."

Our human imagination is tied to our ability to play. We play with ideas, we play with images, we play with possibilities. And, since we are made in the image of the Creator God, we too can create new things. From singing to painting, from weaving to filmmaking, we can enrich the possibilities of human life and the rest of creation.

There are some people whose primary life calling is centered around creation and imagination. These include artists, musicians, dancers, filmmakers, and writers of stories. I will not concentrate on them, for I lack the knowledge or the skill to say much about them or to them.

But, though not many of us are called to be "full-time" artists, just as few are called to be full-time evangelists, we are all called to be artistic, just as we are all called to evangelize. Being creative and imaginative is a vocation not just for artists but for each of us. When we cook, when we dress, when we decorate, when we speak, we are called to do so with God-given imagination. Hence, our first concern here is not with what is in art galleries but with what encircles ordinary life.

We can use almost anything to illustrate our calling to imagination and style, but I would like to focus on something that concerns nearly all of us: how we dress. We get up in the morning and we clothe ourselves in outfits of various colors, shapes, textures, drapes, and patterns. And the way we dress is an aspect of imaging God.

AN ANCIENT FASHION DESIGNER

One of the most remarkable things in the Bible is how many of its most admirable women were involved in the fashion business. At the end of the book of Proverbs is the famous description of a "wife of noble character . . . worth far more than rubies" (Prov. 31:10). This woman does many things, getting up while it is still dark, providing food for the family, giving to the poor, buying fields, and planting vineyards (vv. 15, 16, 20). She runs both the house and the business. She's also something of a gourmet: "She is like the merchant ships, bringing her food from afar" (v. 14).

But what is most commented on in the Bible is what she does with clothes. She "selects wool and flax and works with eager hand" (v. 13). "In her hand she holds the distaff, and grasps the spindle with her fingers" (v. 19). Clearly she knows what to buy and how to spin and weave it. What she makes is not only functional but also beautiful and striking.

She makes bed covers and doesn't worry about the family being cold in the snow because "all of them are clothed in scarlet" (v. 21). Scarlet dye was an expensive commodity, so she'd obviously gone to some pains. Her bedrooms were decorated in the ancient Israelite equivalent of Ralph Lauren. They might even have given Ralph Lauren pause, too, since the bedclothes were scarlet: pretty dramatic. *Better Homes and Gardens* would be interested: "The Scarlet Room: The Noble Woman's Domain." She would also be prepared to meet the photographers when they came calling, for she is "clothed in fine linen and purple" (v. 22). Purple, too, was a difficult to find, high-class dye.

One reason that this woman is so good at what she does is that she doesn't limit herself to providing for the house. She's actually in the garment trade. "She makes linen garments and sells them." It's not just a local trade either—she's tied into the wholesale business, since she "supplied the merchants with sashes" (v. 24).

Obviously, beyond all of these skills, the most important aspect of such a wife is that she fears the Lord (v. 30). All "charm is deception and beauty is fleeting" so that it is her dignity, wisdom, and faith that far outweigh anything else. Nonetheless, her talents are outlined at length and are greeted with high praise. Her fashion sense is depicted as a great and cherished gift of God.

Lest I cause heart attacks among my readers, a few cautions are necessary here. Proverbs is not trying to describe some specific person. It is hard to imagine any one woman being able to do all this, no matter how skilled, hardworking, and faithful she might be. The "Proverbs 31 Woman" is a combination weaver, seamstress, gourmet cook, real estate agent, vineyard manager, social worker, interior decorator, mother, wife, export manager, and all-a-round saint. She makes Supermom look like an underachiever. She makes Martha Stewart look like a bag lady.

It is far more likely that Proverbs gives us a composite picture of all the gifts to be valued in a wife, not a demand that any one human being embody them all. It is a list of accomplishments that are wonderful and desirable in a godly woman, and one of the chief among them is her skill, talent, and imagination as she works with clothing. The Bible tells us that these are things to be greatly desired.

BIBLICAL ARTISTES

This should not surprise us for a second. After all, as we saw, the first person mentioned in the Bible as being "filled . . . with the Spirit of God" was Bezalel, who was gifted "with skill, ability and knowledge in all kinds of crafts" (Exod. 35:31). Bezalel could "make artistic designs for work in gold, silver and bronze, to cut and set stones, to work in wood and to engage in all kinds of artistic craftsmanship" (vv. 32, 33). He was not just a craftsman. He was an artist.

Bezalel, along with Oholiab, was also a good "teacher" (v. 34). They set up training courses to equip people to learn crafts and—

we're back to the fabrics again—designing, weaving, and embroidering in fine linen. All of them were master craftsmen and designers (v. 35).

Now Bezalel & Co. were commissioned to work on the sanctuary and tabernacle that God was building as a home for himself. But this does not mean that such gifts were to be confined to the temple or church. Three points stand out. First, such artistic skills are recognized as gifts from God, as expressions of infilling with the Spirit. Second, God wanted his own house to be graced by human gifts and skills, from gold to embroidery. Third, as the noble wife of Proverbs 31 demonstrates, such skills are also to be used in the service of others. They are gifts for the entire world.

Such skills are also mentioned in relation to women in the early church. In Joppa, there was a woman named Dorcas (also translated Tabitha) who became sick and died. When the disciples heard that Peter was close by, they called for him to come at once. He did, and he raised Dorcas from the dead (see Acts 9:36–42). One intriguing thing is that right after Peter had arrived "all the widows stood around him, crying and showing him the robes that Dorcas had made while she was still with them" (v. 39).

We can safely say that this is not all they talked about—they weren't just grieving because their tailor had gone. They would have discussed her faith, her piety, her service. But, even in their grief and turmoil, they couldn't help but comment on the skill of this pillar of the church. She was obviously a talented woman and Luke, in writing Acts, thought it worthwhile to point this out.

Later on in Acts, we meet Lydia, who opened her heart to God after hearing Paul preach in Philippi (Acts 16:14). She had the disciples come back to stay in her house. Her trade was as "a dealer in purple cloth from the city of Thyatira," a major center for clothing manufacturing. As Mike Starkey says, she was "a rep for a foreign fashion wholesaler."[1]

PURITANIC FASHION PLATES

This pattern of skill in fashion reappears in later Christian history, sometimes in what, for us, seem the most unlikely places. Although the early Protestants, especially the Puritans, are usually regarded as ascetic, fashion-dead killjoys, history reveals exactly the opposite.

General Harrison, part of Cromwell's army, turned up in the English House of Commons in "a scarlet cloak and coat both laden with gold and silver lace, and the coat so covered with cloquant (metal foil) that one scarcely could discern the ground."[2]

Harrison's contemporary, John Owen, was a Puritan's Puritan, and perhaps their greatest and most severe theologian. While Chancellor of Oxford University, he wandered around with "hair powdered, cambric band with large, costly hand strings, velvet jacket, breeches set about at the knees with ribbons pointed, and Spanish leather boots with cambric tops."[3] Today, he'd get thrown out of most Christian colleges even if he were a student, much less the head of the place. He'd probably get thrown out of present-day Oxford as well. There's no accounting for flamboyant Calvinists.

What about the popular image of Puritans decked out in close-fitting black with the occasional white edges? It's true, they often dressed this way, especially on Sundays. But this was no sign of a stifling sobriety or of a rigid desire to suppress any hint of joy or color. Rather it reflected style, especially the better contemporary style of the day. *Black was in*. It was clean lined and elegant.

It had the advantage, especially in church, of not calling foppish attention to oneself but of focusing on God while still celebrating his gifts of clothing and style.

> *Why do we assume that James Dean or Jean-Paul Gaultier wear black out of a sense of style, but the Puritans wore black out of an absence of style? . . . At the fashion shows in October 1993, Calvin Klein unveiled his "New Puritan" look—its clean, straight lines and crisp black and whites prompting the* Independent's *fashion critic to observe that "the clothes of the prayer meeting are on the streets . . ." When the new sophisticated urbanite dons the garb of the Puritan it is considered chic. When the old, unsophisticated Puritan dresses like a Puritan it is considered an absence of chic.[4]*

Calvin, meet Calvin.

CHRISTIAN COUTURE

Does this mean it's no-hold-barred on the clothing front? Can we go out and blow the family budget on the latest duds? Should we hang around fashion shows and take out subscriptions to *GQ* or *Vogue?* The answer is, in a word, no. If we do this, we've missed the essence of Christian culture and Christian couture.

For one thing, clothing (or makeup, or jewelry, or working out so we look good) can become yet another idol. It can become an obsession, or simply something we take too seriously. It can be a source of pride. This is why the Bible is also sharply critical of adornment that reflects vanity. Peter tells the women of his day: "Your beauty should not come from outward adornment, such as braided hair and the wearing of gold jewelry and fine clothes.

Instead, it should be that of your inner self, the unfading beauty of a gentle and quiet spirit, which is of great worth in God's sight" (1 Pet. 3:3–4). The same principles apply to men (see also Ps. 147:10–11; Isa. 3:16–26; Matt. 23:1–12).

The Bible never says that we can't wear fine clothes or concern ourselves with attractive hairstyles or other points of grooming. It is a question of our spirit. Do we go off to church to turn heads? Or do we celebrate God in our dress as we do in our hymns? Church or office, mall or meeting, what is our motivation for looking the way we look?

Nor are the fashions we are to follow necessarily the latest ones out of New York, L.A., or Milan. These can be corrupted and corrupting. I doubt if the mid-nineties wave of decking oneself out like a hooker or a heroin addict reflects the kingdom of God. We can find our own paths. Maybe we can even create our own Christian fashion. Don't laugh—if ghetto baseball caps and grunge rockers can set trends, why can't we?

There are also questions of cost—money and time.

There are hungry people in our world. There are crises in our cities. There are needs in our churches. The fact that clothes (or food or books) are good doesn't mean we have to throw our checkbooks at them. One alternative (one of my favorites) is that we can check out fashion resale shops and consignment stores. My best suit is an Armani. It had been worn about twice and was less expensive than a cheap new one. Frank the tailor did the adjustments for about $20, and I can dress in style for just about any meeting in the world.

But most important, we can discern the biblical spirit. It is neither ostentatious nor showy, neither drab nor utilitarian. It reflects a rich desire that the way we live, the way we dress, the way we use texture and color and shape celebrate the richness of God's world and express the imagination with which he has endowed us.[5] A Christian approach to fashion is neither spend-thrift nor miserly. Like the pattern of frugality and feast in the life of Israel, it knows how to conserve, and how to celebrate. It knows that there are times of restraint and times to let go (see Isa. 61:10, 11). It knows both poverty and riches.

> *The crowning irony is that many of the poorest people of the world are those who most value ornament, beauty and celebration. Any encounter with the bright, vibrant fabrics, the fabulous jewelry, and the strong heritage of dance and ritual in traditional Africa leaves one in little doubt whether it is African culture or our own which is the more impoverished. Or try telling a proud Asian father who has saved up for a lifetime for his daughter's dowry, and who wishes to see her (if only for one day) as a princess, that he is wrong.[6]*

I've dwelt at length on clothing not because it is the only or the most important expression of artistic imagination. It is simply something with which we all live and, for most of us, something about which we make choices every day. These same themes affect other parts of our lives as well: the ways we wor-ship, the ways we do business, the ways we eat, the ways we write and speak. These, too, should benefit from our God-given creativity and imagination.

FOOD WITH STYLE

Just as clothing is not only to keep us warm and dry, so food is not only a means to keep us fed. For those of us with enough to eat, food doesn't just fill us up, it tastes good. If done well, it delights us. We savor its texture, its flavor, its aroma. Choosing foods and cooking requires imagination as well as skill. In most cultures around the world, a celebration is also a feast. If we're going to eat well, special dishes require a long time cooking. We aren't usually satisfied with gray tasteless sludge, which merely takes away the pangs of hunger. We seek a delight for eye and tongue, imparting a gladness to be in the world.

This too can be overdone. Some people in the world don't have much choice about what they get to eat, or how, or if, it is prepared. And if we, like much of North American culture, totally separate eating from the needs of hunger, we'll end up fat. But food too is a gift of God, and a calling to imaginative stewardship beyond mere utility. As Calvin wrote,

> *If we consider to what end God created foods, we shall find that he wished not only to provide for our necessities, but also for our pleasure and recreation. . . . With herbs, trees and fruits, besides the various uses he gives us of them, it was his will to rejoice our sight by their beauty, and to give us yet another pleasure in their odours. . . . Lastly, has he not given us many things which we ought to hold in esteem without their being necessary to us?*

SPEAKING WITH STYLE

Even the act of speaking calls for creative energy. Do we just go on in a droning voice, or do we speak with inflection and vigor? Are our words flat and repetitive? Is our only positive adjective "nice"? Calvin Seerveld makes the point that one reason there is so much swearing in North America is that people have lost the ability to use words, to say with passion and emphasis what they mean. In this situation, the only way to emphasize a point, to express anger or delight, is "F" this and "F" that. The one who swears has only about three words available to express anything other than the time of day.[7]

The solution to this is not that we become wordsmiths, capable of dropping Shakespearean allusions and antique verbs into every sentence, any more than that we should all become fashion designers or gourmet cooks. It is that we realize that God wants our clothing, our food, our speech, and every single thing that we do to be a response of creative, imaginative, stylish, and joyful creatures.

This can have many good effects. A church that has style appeals to people. A preacher who preaches both with the power of faith and the splendor of words draws people. A church that cooks well attracts people.

Prince Edward Island in Canada is beautiful. Its rich red soil and deep green fields are dotted with pristine, white farms. Miles of white sand beaches touch water crawling with luscious lobsters. The stories of Anne of Green Gables were set here, which is the main reason that three times a week, 747's loaded with Japanese tourists land at Charlottetown's tiny airport after a direct flight from Tokyo.

PEI is small, and its hotels and restaurants cannot handle all of the summer tourist rush, so local churches have taken up the slack by serving meals to tourists. They make lobster suppers, and fabulous ones. The women who prepare the food have been doing so for years, and Parisian chefs would have little to teach them and much to learn from them.

The suppers are served not only on Sundays, but every night of the week, and the locals and tourist guides know how to judge them. You've got to book early—Friday supper in St. Peter's church basement can be the toughest place in town to get a reservation.

Do the hungry tourists get closer to the gospel by eating in the churches? Maybe, maybe not. But they will certainly receive a good gift from God—great food. And their view of the church will be changed, perhaps so subtly that they will not even realize it. Somewhere, at least, Christians know how to cook well, and even if for that reason alone others choose to be with them, churches will be places of happy memory.

WORKING FOR THE MASTER

Whether we are bona fide artists or musicians or mere strugglers trying to bring some life and nuance to our circumstances, we are developing gifts in the kingdom of God. As we create—paintings or symphonies, sculptures or novels, photographs or architecture, wardrobe ensembles or feasts, words of wisdom or words of wit—we mirror, in small portion, the genius of our Creator. As we work, we offer our best and our brightest work as a gift to him who created us in his image, for his honor, and for his delight. And whether we are professional artists or simply Christians who create for the joy of it, we are performing, most of all, for the "Master of all Good Workmen," who will keep us creating forever. Rudyard Kipling's phrasing is old, but his vision is timeless.

When Earth's last picture is painted and the tubes are twisted and dried,

*When the oldest colors have faded, and the youngest critic
   has died,*

*We shall rest, and, faith, we shall need it—lie down for an aeon
   or two,*

Till the Master of All Good Workmen shall put us to work anew!

*And those that were good shall be happy; they shall sit in a
   golden chair;*

*They shall splash at a ten-league canvas with brushes of
   comets' hair.*

*They shall find real saints to draw from—Magdalene, Peter
   and Paul;*

They shall work for an age at a sitting and never be tired at all.

*And only the Master shall praise us, and only the Master
   shall blame;*

*And no one shall work for money, and no one shall work
   for fame,*

*But each for the joy of the working, and each, in his separate
   star,*

*Shall draw the Thing as he sees It for the God of Things as They
   Are!*

—Rudyard Kipling,
"When Earth's Last Picture Is Painted"

twelve

CREATIVITY AND TECHNOLOGY

Geologists are usually schizophrenic. At least, exploration geologists usually are. Most people get into this line of work because they love being out in the boonies. Why would you spend half your life in a tent watching the snow come down in August, discovering that horse flies can be two inches long, or debating the fact that grizzly bears are the world's largest land carnivores and that they're out there, now, on the loose, and hungry?

You do it because you can go to places that others only dream about (or pay small fortunes to reach). You do it because there is no sight like velvet-edged stars on an arctic night. Because you can watch the dawn over pink-tipped icy peaks and hear the crack of deep blue, brilliant glaciers. Because you can sit and contemplate a moose, who stands and contemplates you, unafraid, because you are the first person it has ever seen. Because you can walk for hours, alone, and watch the mountain ridges stretch beyond the bounds of the world. You can hear the deepest silence and breathe the purest air.

But why else are you there? Why does someone spend thousands of dollars for a helicopter to move you around? Why does someone actually pay you to do this, to be in the land of your dreams? Why? Because you are there to look at soils and rocks and minerals. And if you look well, and if you are lucky, there will soon be drilling rigs there. And if that is successful, there will be a well or a mine. There will be mills or pipelines, heaps of tailings and lumps of earth. The air will echo with the snarl of machines, the animals will flee or die, and scars will appear over the face of the land.

If you are successful, you will have a small part in destroying that which you love. Your function in being there is to end that which draws you there. Herein lies your schizophrenia. You escape the technological society only by being its advance guard.

There is no easy way out of this vise. Even when we discount our waste, our twisted motives, and our unthinking exploitation, we still need minerals. This dilemma does not exist only because of sin; it is a fundamental part of the nature of our existence. Our lives as persons and as societies involve real and costly decisions—a weighing and stewarding of real losses and gains. The way we do that now is often idolatrous and cruel, of course, but even doing it properly will not answer all the questions.

TECHNOLOGICAL DREAMS AND NIGHTMARES

The word *technology* conjures up thrilling visions: the brilliant illusions of "Star Wars"; pictures of men on the moon beamed direct to the living room; computers and the Internet; robots; lasers; genetic engineering; heart transplants; cloning. Slightly more mundanely, we can fly the length of the country in a few hours, buy food from around the world in our local store, show movies on our own TV, and light and heat our homes at the flick of a switch.

Darker visions also come: assembly lines reducing the lives of women and men to inhuman rhythms; poisoned rivers and stripped forests; unwelcome surveillance of our lives; mammoth, distant organizations.

Technology brings promise and fate, blessing and curse. Those of us reading this book have been liberated from the life of peasants. Our working day has been reduced in length; the number of our choices has increased. At the same time, the social world has become more massive and alien, and we do not know if the world we are re-creating is one that can or will ultimately sustain healthy human (and non-human) life.

But technology is not just a "thing" out there, totally separate from us. Technology contains both good and evil—and in this it reflects the fact that it is something we humans create. Technology is human desire and human society writ large, or writ small.

There are many problems with technology. It can destroy the landscape and corrupt human life. But to believe that we can abandon the skills we have learned and all the machines that we have built is to engage in a fantasy. We now live longer, we are healthier, we have more opportunities, and we enjoy a more varied life. Most of those who denounce technology have no real desire to live in some primitive civilization. Instead, many of them sit amidst the fruits of technical progress all the while denouncing the technology that brought them. Technology, properly used, is a gift from God.

The topic of technique and technology preoccupies today's world. Technique refers to "how to" do something—it is the science of "how." It encompasses all that we can do—from going to the moon to public speaking, from designing nuclear bombs to making love, from serving a hungry neighbor to writing books. All of these are included when we talk about technique.

Along with technique comes technology, which is the made, created, embodied structure of technique. Technology includes, in one form or another, *all* those things that do not naturally occur, all those things that we shape and reshape. Technology infuses art as much as physics, families as much as engineering. To talk about technique and technology is to talk in one particular way about all of human life, as all of human life has some technical aspect. Responsible technical skill is both a gift and a calling. It is the human task of reshaping the materials of God's world in new ways. It is imagination and skill in the service of usefulness.

TECHNOLOGY AND HUMAN RESPONSIBILITY

This element of human responsibility is always manifest to us in the Scriptures. The Bible shows the curse that is upon those who do evil, those who serve false gods; but it also shows us the blessing, the *shalom*, upon those who serve God and live justly, stewardly, and faithfully. And this curse and blessing is also shown in technology.

One of the most remarkable things about Genesis is *how much* responsibility human beings are given. For example, God gave Adam the power and authority to name the animals. It was not as if the animals already really had names that had been given by God and that Adam was simply to discern and announce. It wasn't a game: God had left the names completely open.

Adam *gave* names to the animals (Gen. 2:20). God himself *did not know* what the names would be; he wanted "to see what he [Adam] would name them" (v. 19). Adam had full authority to give these names so that "whatever the man called each living creature, that was its name" (v. 20). This was now the name that everyone would use—even God. Henceforth God would be directed by Adam's decision. Adam was not just finding and following a set of rules. He was shaping something new and giving identity to the world.

As we saw earlier, our human task in the world is concerned not only with preserving the creation, though we must certainly do that. It is also concerned with making the creation *fruitful*, with helping it grow, with giving it shape.

Nor is our task in the world simply following the clear rules that God has set down, though we must certainly follow God's commandments and learn from the creation itself. We have a creative task in the world. We must shape things in ways for which there is sometimes no clear direction. This is why imagination is not just a feature of the arts; it is a feature of human life itself. Without imagination, without experimentation, without openness to new questions and new possibilities, there can be no science and no technology. We are not challenging God when we do this, at least not when we do it in humility and faith. We are not stealing fire from the gods. We are taking up our responsibility before God to shape what he has placed in our hands.

TECHNOLOGY: THE ANSWER TO ALL QUESTIONS?

Modern society has two contradictory attitudes toward technology. One is applause for a brilliant technological future. Many of our scientists and politicians seem to be trapped in a view that technology can solve everything. Bad health? We need more medicine. Lousy education? We need more computers. Depressed people? We need more therapists. Growing crime? We need better police systems. Environmental problems? We need more efficient clean-up procedures. Behind these views lies a primitive science-fiction type of worldview—if we can learn how to control and manipulate nature well enough, we will all be free and happy. The social scientists wade in also—if we can find out what factors determine people's lives, we can produce happy, healthy, integrated people.

The point here is not that computers or clean-up technology or social science are bad. They can all be very useful and should be used. *But if we think we can address the fundamental problems of humankind without addressing human guilt, human responsibility, human morality, and the reality of human freedom, then we are living in a dream world*: we are insane. We are out of touch with reality. (The gospel tells us what *reality* is—what this world is really like, and what "works"—not just in a "spiritual" realm but in concrete everyday life.)

Because of the helplessness of our science and technology to address many of the problems that actually keep most of us awake at night, our society also swings to the opposite extreme. Just as we have a reaction that says that human beings should never, ever, interfere with the "natural" order, so we have a reaction that claims that human technical power is *always* destructive and, so, we must somehow revert to a more primitive form of existence.

Both views are wrong. The "technology-is-the-key" view is off target because it sees problems only as challenges to be conquered and never to be accepted with humility. The "technology-is-the-problem" view is wrong because it sees technology only as a means of domination, never of service.

The Bible certainly talks of the good and bad of technology. On the one hand it condemns science and technology driven by human pride. It shows the dark side of technology.

The line of technical development is first followed through the genealogy of Cain. It is Cain himself who builds the first city (see Gen. 4:17). Later the tower of Babel "with its top in the heavens," the greatest architectural achievement of humans, is portrayed as the culmination of sin. The fall of Adam and Eve is replayed at Babel as a lust for power and greatness that over-reaches human limitations. People thought that their skill could make them gods. The result was that they no longer understood one another; they were driven apart, and hated one another (see Gen. 11:1–10).

The prophets developed part of this theme. They always linked any achievement, artistic, cultural, or technical, with the way it had come into being. They did not accept as beautiful that which has been created through pride, oppression, or injustice. Habbakuk says: "Woe to him who builds a city with bloodshed and establishes a town by crime! . . . the nations exhaust themselves for nothing" (Hab. 12:12).

Isaiah concurs,

The LORD Almighty has a day in store for all the proud and lofty,
for all that is exalted (and they will be humbled),
for all the cedars of Lebanon, tall and lofty, and all the oaks of
   Bashan,
for all the towering mountains and all the high hills,
for every lofty tower and every fortified wall,
for every trading ship and every stately vessel.
The arrogance of man will be brought low and the pride of men
   humbled; the LORD alone will be exalted in that day,
and the idols will totally disappear.
Men will flee to caves in the rocks and to holes in the ground from
   dread of the LORD and the splendor of his majesty, when he rises
   to shake the earth.
In that day men will throw away to the rodents and bats their
   idols of silver and idols of gold, which they made to worship.
They will flee to caverns in the rocks and to the overhanging crags
   from dread of the LORD and the splendor of his majesty, when
   he rises to shake the earth.

Isaiah 2:12–21

Those that trust in technology will find themselves betrayed by their idol; they will live in caves and holes with bats and rats.

The Bible never condemns technology itself. It describes the human development of musical instruments, of bricks, and herding. It places human beings as creators within the creation. It does not make the modern distinction between what is "natural" and what is "artificial." Both are seen merely as aspects of what is "creational," a category that includes both the human and the non-human world in relation to each other. Technology itself is good, but in human hands it can become a curse. This means that the modern world calls upon us as Christians to emphasize the theme of *responsibility* in technology, and this can be a difficult and demanding calling.

We are a technically proficient people. We can build tall buildings, wide bridges, and huge dams. But there are some things that we can no longer do. For one thing, we've lost the ability to build great cathedrals. It's not really a matter of the skills required, though it would be very hard to find the stone masons and expert carvers. It's more a matter, like everything important, of the spirit.

A LEGACY OF CREATIVITY

We don't know the names of the great builders and craftsmen who created the great gothic cathedrals of Europe. They didn't carve their names in what they built, and they left no separate record so that their fame could be established. The cathedrals themselves were the memory they wished to leave behind.

These cathedrals took several generations to build. Those who began to build them knew that they would never see the completed structure. They immersed themselves and all their energy, labor, and skill on a project they themselves would never see. When they died, there would merely be piles of unfinished masonry beginning their climb into the sky.

Anyone building such a cathedral would have to have been at the peak of his profession and have possessed enough spiritual discipline to labor anonymously for something that he would never see completed. It meant self-abnegation, self-sacrifice to a degree unheard of in this day and age. Our greatest barrier is not our ingenuity. It is our egos. And no amount of technology can overcome this.

MODERN TECHNOLOGY

The structure of modern technology means that all of our designs are interconnected. We can't just try to be responsible for what we do with this machine today, we have to wrestle with the overall pattern of our society. We no longer use a tool or a machine arbitrarily in some small area of an otherwise natural or personal world. We are not primarily using a plough or a tractor in the midst of a field. We are not simply using a technical thing in the midst of a non-technical world.

Rather, we now use technology as a part of a world *that is itself shaped and made by past and present technology*. We use a stove in the kitchen. We operate laboratories at the pinnacle of a technical education system. We have auto assembly lines in the middle of factories, served by technically trained employees, at the nexus of a network of roads, fed by the transport of raw material, as part of an overall production process, linked with other factories and mines and dealers and drivers, carried on in the framework of technical laws and regulations and specifications developed to cope with it.

We live and act within a technically shaped world, one that in turn shapes and limits what we do. We make decisions and we act within the possible choices and options presented to us by a world that we (or others) have *already* shaped, opened, or constricted by our previous actions and techniques. When we use a tool, we shape a world, but it in return shapes not only what we do but also what we *can* do.

The structure of modern technology shows that technologies are never "neutral"—they are not just tools that happen to be lying around, which we can use at will for either good or evil purposes. They become part of the structure of the world in which we live, part of the pattern of our lives. Technologies always embody, promote, and reproduce human commitments, beliefs, and activities; they can free us or trap us by what we have already done; they can reduce our actions and our futures to mere extrapolations, extensions of our past. Technologies are both cages and doors.

COMPUTERS: MORE THAN MEETS THE EYE

This constricting nature of modern technology can be shown in the example of computers. Computers can be used for bad purposes—keeping track of political enemies, spreading pornography on the Internet, or dehumanizing offices and banks. Computers can also be used for good things—making word processing easier, keeping track of records, searching masses of data of key information, and replacing boring or repetitive human work. Indeed many of our other new scientific and technological developments would be impossible without computers.

Does this mean that the computer doesn't shape us and mold us? Does it mean that it's really only a question of how *we* decide to use it? Not at all—for *a computer is much more than what it does*. Consider:

If we want to use computers, we have to be able to *make* computers. Therefore we have to have factories making silicon chips and other factories refining materials to a very high order of purity. We must have metallurgical facilities, we must have mills, we must have mines, we must have roads, and we must have electricity.

If we want to use computers, we must have *people* who can make them and program them. We must have high-level mathematical and engineering skills. We must have trained graduates. We must have universities and technical schools that can produce them. In turn, we must have high schools to feed these, and grade schools to feed the high schools, and parents to encourage the children.

If we want to use computers, we must have things to use them *for*. We must have markets, which means that *many* governments, firms, and people have to use them. Patterns of business, work, research, and communication must to be re-adapted for computer use. If we wish to use a computer, then we must have more than one of them. We must make them widespread throughout the society.

Clearly, we can't just use computers for worthwhile ends and assume that this affects nothing else. *If we decide, consciously or unconsciously, to use computers, we have already, of absolute necessity, dictated a large part of what our economics, communications, government, education, and social patterns are going to be like.*

A decision for computers is inevitably a decision about what sort of society we are going to live in: it *must be* the sort of society that can sustain computers. The same is true with any technological development, even the most basic. An archaeologist discovering a tool can tell you a great deal about what the society it came from must have been like in order for it to have used that particular tool. When we use any technology we, in large part, determine what our world will be like.

SHAPING AND RESHAPING OUR WORLD

As we determine what our world will be like, our lives and choices will determine what *we* will be like. Our goals, hopes, fears, faiths, and expectations will be reshaped. For example, how many of us go home for lunch at lunchtime? How many of us even think about it? We don't think about it because, for most of us, it has become virtually impossible. Going home for lunch is no longer part of our world.

Of course, not so long ago, many of us went home for lunch, and so did our children. We didn't take it for granted that the family would have to be apart for the entire working day. But gradually we lost that benefit, usually without even noticing it. Now we know, without even thinking about it, that we work too far away. The buses aren't convenient, and traffic is a problem. We don't even try to go home at noon anymore; we just face up to the "reality"—a "reality" that we have slowly helped to create both without realizing it and without counting its cost. We don't even feel a loss of freedom, for the new sense of reality has gradually seeped even into our unconscious minds.

So it is that when we shape the world, we shape ourselves. We open up new possibilities for life, but we close down others. The world we are shaping and have shaped becomes what we now call "reality," and, of course, we must be "realistic." So we adjust and accommodate ourselves to what we have made, and we do not think about what we have lost. We begin to remake ourselves in the image of our technology and, if that is deficient or unjust, then we become deficient and unjust, too. When our technology is idolatrous, those idols will control us.

How are we to respond to this situation? By rejecting technology? Certainly not, for, as I have tried to show, God has made us creatures who refine, who shape, who create. We need technical developments, and even if we sought to reject them, we would make them anyway.

But what we must do is break with the *idol* of technology—the idea that we can achieve health, wealth, happiness, and security through it. We must break with the idea that expertise is the key to solving all problems and with the idea that human freedom comes from human control. We must break with the urge that drives us to accept the more sophisticated as the better, the hope that identifies progress with technical accomplishments, the vision that says humans can be brought to fulfillment by manipulating them as we would manipulate objects.

Breaking away from such an idol is different from and much more than "finding new values"—as if we could just decide, arbitrarily, to want something else instead. We cannot "make" new values or "find" them as if they lay about us just waiting to be picked up. An idol is fundamentally religious, and we truly need, both as persons and as a society, a religious conversion in our relation to technology.

We must believe, day by day, within our factories, workshops, and laboratories, that technology is a means, not an end, a servant, not a promise. We must hold on to the reality that the kingdom of heaven is promised to the poor in spirit, that the pure in heart shall see God, that the meek *really will* inherit the earth. These are not moral norms for some distant transcendent realm; they are the most fundamental and realistic touchstones for our entire everyday lives, including our development of technology.

In so doing we will no longer need to be driven by the work of our hands. And in so doing, we can rejoice in our wealth of technical skills and expertise. We can liberate technology even as we are liberated from it.

Across the sea from Culion lies the island of Coron Reef, one of the most beautiful and mysterious islands in the world.

Coron Reef is an old coral reef, which has now been raised above the surrounding ocean. Its sheer, white walls of shimmering coral rise hundreds of feet into the air. Scattered in untamed abundance over the cliffs are luscious green plants, including wild jade trees. Flying above the water's edge are parrots and kingfishers calling out to one another, their voices echoing along the silent cliffs. Beyond the occasional break in the coral walls are inlets that glow like jewels, their blue waters lapping against the white sand.

The island itself is a jagged and raw profusion of knife-edged vertical rocks that impede human movement—it can take an hour to travel fifty feet. In the interior are hidden mystic lakes and tribal peoples who climb the cliffs to collect birds' nests.

Around the edges of the island are occasional strips of beach where native peoples live beneath the cliffs and overhanging trees in thatched huts, fishing for their food. If ever there were an image of human beings living simply and in harmony with the natural world, this would be it.

But life here is neither simple nor easy nor harmonious. The food supplies are limited. The problem is not the quantity of food but its range. Vitamin deficiency is common. Many of the children have straw blond hair, which looks exotic to visitors but is actually a sign of severe malnutrition. Their eyes are dull and lifeless. And the fishing itself is dangerous and, at times, fruitless.

Life on this island is hard and very, very short. The people desperately need medical attention. While we were there they asked to serve as our guides in trade for gasoline, since using a small motor is many times better than trying to paddle endlessly against the contrary sea. Theirs is no Polynesian paradise of uncorrupted harmony, no escape from our harried, dehumanized technical world. They envy us our "easy" way of life, which seems so much better than their never-ending struggle for survival beneath the green-jeweled cliffs.

OUR HOPE

FOR THE WORLD

PART V

thirteen

WORSHIP AND IDOLATRY

Early one morning I walked along a ridge in the then "homeland"
of Ciskei in South Africa. In the distance the morning mists were
beginning to clear, and the early light of the sun was catching the
snow-edged peaks in purple light. Below me, still in shadow, lay a
small, scattered village. Cooking fires were burning, and the
smoke rose in slim spirals in the still morning air until they
merged to form a sweet-smelling haze of woodsmoke that lay pro-
tectively over the village.

Like the smoke, a song also enveloped the village, a slow
melody that rose and fell as the day brightened. I could see figures
emerge from the huts and then draw breath to join in the morn-
ing song. As they walked, swaying elegantly, carrying clothing or
wood or food, they continued to sing until, when they entered
another hut, they ceased. But the song itself never stopped. As dif-
ferent people appeared, they sang. Though the singers varied,
there were always people present to join in the song. It seemed that
even if none of the people sang, even if they were all silent, the
song would somehow remain, echoing peacefully up the valley.

It was as though the song itself had a life of its own. Like the smoke, it hung over the village, and people could join in or withdraw from it, but it would still be there. It existed before them, and they were part of it. It was not so much that they had decided to begin singing but that they were joining a song that was given to them in the fabric of the creation itself.

WORSHIP AS THE HEART OF LIFE

The creation itself worships God: "The heavens declare the glory of God; the skies proclaim the work of his hands" (Ps. 19:1). And when we worship, we join in that song. We touch the core of our existence as human beings. When we are called to worship, we do not so much create something ourselves; rather, we more clearly recognize and join the creation's praise to the God who is always with it and with us.

Worship is spiritual in the sense that it is from our spirit, from the core of our being. But it is not spiritual in the sense of being disembodied. Worship is fully physical as well as fully spiritual: in the Old Testament, we find bowing, kneeling, falling down, lifted hands, and leaps of celebration as part of worship (see Pss. 5:7; 44:25; 63:4; 95:6; 2 Sam. 6:14–16, 21; Dan. 8:17–18). In the New Testament, Paul encouraged lifting up of hands, Jesus knelt, and the father danced at the return of the prodigal son (see Matt. 26:39; Luke 15:11–31; 22:41; 1 Tim. 2:8).[1]

Apart from all these, of course, we pray, loudly or quietly; we preach; and like the rest of the creation, we sing. Our worship is simultaneously bodily and spiritual as we worship the one who himself took on human flesh, became a man, lived and walked among us, died for us, and rose in the body for us.

There is nothing unearthly or un-creational about <u>worship</u>. It is not a time apart; it is a time within. It is not a time withdrawn; it is a time fully involved. <u>It is not a time when we shed our human selves; it is a time when we are most fully human.</u> <u>It is the recognition and restoration of our relation with God, which lies at the center of the world.</u> And when we worship the Lord, we are also refusing to worship—to make ultimate—the things about us, or to deify ourselves or our gifts. We look beyond the good creation to the Creator himself. We touch the source of our lives, our hopes, and our salvation.

Worship does not take us to a realm beyond human life but to the heart of human life. In worship we commune with God who is the core of our existence and the source of our hope. In genuine worship, we meet the one who has created and redeemed the world, and through genuine worship we also begin to see the world as it really is and should be seen. Worship is no more sacred, per se, than doing dishes or playing with children. But it is the center of life, without which everything else would, as surely as night follows day, disintegrate and perish.

Since every human hope, dream, word, song, plan, event, work, or action can be service to God, we should be very careful about dividing up the world into parts that are "religious" and parts that are not. *Everything* done in the right way and in the right spirit is a part of our faith. In the same way, everything (even prayer and worship) that is done in the wrong way and in the wrong spirit can be an expression of sin. Both sin and holiness permeate every dimension of our lives. Prayer may be blasphemous, and bricklaying may be holy. Sermons may be treacherous, and jokes may be healing. The question is, who or what do they serve: ourselves, the things in the world, or the Lord God Almighty? The true God, or an idol?

GOD OR IDOLS?

We should never consider people, corporations, books, or governments as "non-religious." They are always religious in that they reflect in their beliefs, thoughts, words, and acts either a turning toward God, or a turning away from God, or a bit of both. As one friend remarked, "I can tell more about your faith from reading your checkbook than your prayer book." Our checkbooks show what we think is most important. Where our money is, there also is our heart.

As a popular Bob Dylan song pointed out, "You Gotta Serve Somebody." Everybody serves somebody. If we do not serve God, then we will serve something else. The "somethings" that people serve are what the Bible calls "idols."

The history of Israel is full of references to "idols," "graven images," and "high places." Israel's sin was always evidenced by its turning away from God and turning to idols. We might even say that idolatry is not just another sin alongside the rest, but is one particular way of speaking about all sin. This is because *all sin is an expression of the basic sin of idolatry, of putting something else in the place of God.* As the old Sunday school illustration rightly asks, "Who is on the throne of your life—Christ or you?" This is one reason why idolatry is condemned in the very first of the Ten Commandments: "You shall have no other gods besides me. You shall not make for yourselves a graven image" (Exod. 20:3, 4).

In the Scriptures no one is described as a non-believer: rather, people are described in terms of what they *do* believe. If someone does not worship and serve the true God, then he or she will inevitably worship and serve another "god." We always serve what we worship and worship what we truly serve. The other "gods" we are tempted to serve are things within the creation. They can be things already put there by God, such as trees or rocks or fish or sex, or else things made by human hands, such as machines or possessions or armies or knowledge. *In idolatry, instead of treating the creation only as a good gift of God, we give it the place of God.* Whenever we hold something apart from God to be the core or key to our problems, we make an idol.

IN WHOM DO WE TRUST?

Habakkuk says, "What profit is an idol when its maker has shaped it, a metal image, a teacher of lies? *For the workman trusts in his own creation when he makes dumb idols*" (2:18, emphasis added). Paul describes idols as "a representation by the art and the imagination of man" (Acts 17:29), and he condemns "worshiping the creature rather than the creator" (Rom. 1:24). Idolatry is trusting in our own creation, our own imagination, our own skill, our own work.

WORSHIPING AT THE ALTAR OF SECURITY

The worship of idols, like the worship of God, is never, ever a purely formal matter, like having a little shrine in the living room. Worship, whether true or idolatrous, is reflected in what we do every day of our lives, in where we put our hearts, minds, and bodies. This is why Paul describes true worship as "renewing our minds" (Rom. 12:2) and James describes true religion as "caring for widows and orphans" (James 1:27). Idolatry can be manifested in many ways. When the prophets spoke of it, idolatry was often associated with acts of pride and oppression. Isaiah says,

> *For thou hast rejected thy people, the house of Jacob, because they are full of diviners from the east and soothsayers like the Philistines, and they strike hands with foreigners. Their land is filled with silver and gold, and there is no end to their treasures; their land is filled with horses, and there is no end to their chariots. Their land is filled with idols;* they bow down to the works of their hands, to what their fingers have made.
>
> Isaiah 2:6–8 (emphasis added)

The sins listed by Isaiah are all different ways of turning away from God.

The house of Jacob gave heed to false gods (through diviners and soothsayers) and thought fortune telling, or future telling, or futurology, or social science was the key to security. If the people knew what the future held, they wouldn't have to worry.

By compromising with foreigners, the house of Jacob picked up ways other than the ways God had taught them. They thought that by making treaties with strong powers such as the Egyptians or the Babylonians, their future would be secure.

The house of Jacob sought wealth and security (gold and silver) rather than God. They thought that if they had enough money and goods, then nothing could harm them.

The house of Jacob relied on military might (chariots—the means of attack, the means of aggressive, not defensive, warfare) rather than God. Israel was allowed by God to defend itself but not to attack others. But the house of Jacob thought that if they had chariots, the most advanced weapons of the time, then nothing could threaten them.

All these are different ways of believing that something *within* the world is the key to our security and happiness. This is why, when Isaiah ends the list by saying "the land is filled with idols," he is not really adding *another* item to the list. Rather, he is *summarizing* the central theme of the whole list. *He is showing the sin that lies at the heart of all other sins.* The diviners, the treaties with foreigners, the gold and the chariots are *themselves* the idols, because *they* are what Israel trusts, rather than trusting in God.

Therefore, just as Habakkuk condemns the workman "trusting in his own creation" (2:18), so Isaiah condemns "trust in chariots" (31:1). Military power can be an idol as potent—or as useless—as Baal, Moloch, or Ashtaroth. The worship of money, the act of relying on money for peace or health, is mammon worship. And Jesus says, "No man can worship two masters" (Matt. 6:24).

Idolatry is not something that happened only in ancient times or in faraway places; it happens *now*, everywhere. It was not just a sin of Israel, or of supposedly "primitive" peoples—it is a sin of Americans and everyone else. We must look at the supposedly scientific, secular, and rational world about us with this understanding of idols squarely in mind. Many people deeply believe, trust way down in their hearts, even put their lives on the line, hoping that mere military power will bring peace, or that mere science will solve our problems, or that mere wealth will bring happiness, or that mere education will bring tolerance. Then we will echo Paul's cry to the philosophers on Mars Hill in Athens who thought that they were so deeply rational and beyond all religion and superstition: "I perceive that in every way you are very religious" (Acts 17:22).

None of this means that the things we idolize are, in themselves, necessarily bad. Legitimate military defense, money, learning, and work are not inherently wrong. But it doesn't matter whether they are good or bad. The key to idolatry is the faith that *we ourselves* put in something. We can make *any* good gift of God—sex, wealth, nature, science, education, work, or skill—into an idol if we put our ultimate trust in it. Then that good thing will be turned to evil.

Everything in the creation is given for our good and is meant to be used rightly to bring blessing. But *none* of them can be the final cause of hope, or the foundation of peace, or the source of love. *None* of them can be trusted in or relied upon for our ultimate salvation. *All* of them find their proper place only when we humbly rely upon God's faithfulness, justice, and mercy.

IN THE IMAGE OF OUR IDOLS

Idols, ancient and modern, always have an effect upon those that worship them. Our relations with idols do not just go one way—from us to them. They go both ways—from us to them and back again. We are shaped by our idols. The psalmist describes this effect: "The idols of the nations are silver and gold, the work of men's hands. They have mouths but they speak not, they have ears but they hear not, they have eyes but they see not, nor is there any breath in their mouths. *Those that trust in them are like them!* Yea, everyone who trusts in them" (Ps. 135:15–18, emphasis added).

As the psalmist says, *we become like our idols*. We create them, but then we, in turn, become transformed into their image. In a way, this is a reflection of a more basic law: *we become like whatever we worship*. If we worship God in heart and soul and mind and truth, then we will become ever more transformed into his image. If we worship an idol, we will be transformed into its image. Ralph Waldo Emerson expressed this well:

> *The Gods we worship write their names on our faces; be sure of that. And a man will worship something—have no doubts about that, either. He may think that his tribute is paid in secret in the dark recesses of his heart—but it will out. That which dominates will determine his life and character. Therefore, it behooves us to be careful what we worship, for what we are worshipping we are becoming.*[2]

The effect of worship does not even stop there, for we human beings are in daily contact with one another and the world. We are the stewards of the earth, the shapers of human life and culture. Since our worship shapes who we are, it also shapes what we create. As we are the shapers of society, then necessarily and inevitably we will shape our society into the pattern of our worship, either of the false "gods," idols, or of the true God. In whatever we build or create or shape, we are giving expression to the intentions and hopes of our hearts, to what we most deeply believe, to what we ultimately trust. Our daily life together, our organizations, our habits, our machines, our education, our political life, all will bear the mark of our worship.

From his own studies of idolatry in society, Christian economist Bob Goudzwaard suggests three general principles to explain the connection between our worship of God or "gods" and the society we create.[3] Goudzwaard develops the meaning of idolatry and discusses the modern idols of "nation," "revolution," "material prosperity," and "guaranteed security" in his *Idols of Our Time*. The principles are:

1. People serve god(s) with their lives.

2. People are transformed into an image of their god.

3. Mankind creates and forms a structure of society in its own image and, hence, into the image of its idols.[4]

ADDICTIONS AND PERSONAL IDOLS

The process of drug addiction may be used to illustrate the effect of idols on an individual life. Initially the drug, whether it might be cigarettes, alcohol, or cocaine, has no power over the user. He or she can usually easily decide whether to use it again, for in the early stages the power of the drug is still relatively weak. Often people don't even like its effects the first few times and have to really work at getting into it.

But as the user continues to give in to the addiction, there is a gradual transfer of power to the drug, sometimes too subtle for the user even to discern. After a period of months or years it can become almost impossible to break away, to smash the hold it has over life. Many addicts will face death rather than relinquish their drug. In this regard, drug addiction is like idolatry, for we will give up everything—jobs, families, homes, hopes, dreams, even life itself, rather than surrender our idols. As Richard Mouw puts it, every alcoholic at some point sings his own version of Martin Luther's great hymn: "Let goods and kindred go; this mortal life also; I'm going to get loaded."[5]

What is the source of this power—a power sometimes of life or death? A drug such as nicotine or cocaine is harmless if it merely sits on the table. It cannot reach out and grab us by the throat. In fact the power that it exercises is a power that only comes *from us* when we give ourselves to it. But, as we reach out, gradually this power is transferred until the drug has power over us.

This is the structure of idolatry: when something without power in itself becomes the obsessive focus of human commitment, it begins to exercise power over us. The non-gods begin to act like gods. This is one reason why the Bible at times says that idols are dead, lifeless, and powerless (see Ps. 135:15–18) and at other times seems to say that they have power.[6]

IDOLATROUS "CITY CENTERS"

The effect of idols is present not only in our individual lives but also in our societies. The central focus of our social lives can be shown even in our cities. Cities come, of course, in all shapes, sizes, and rhythms. But the structure of cities is not random or haphazard, even if they are not officially planned. People usually put what they value most right at the center of their lives. In turn, the most valuable buildings are usually put on the most valuable real estate. And in cities, the most valuable real estate has usually been in the center. Therefore, as a very general rule of thumb, we will usually find what a culture values most highly by observing what is housed in the buildings that lie at the heart of its cities.

As literary critic Northrop Frye has pointed out, "In what our culture produces, whether it is art, philosophy, military strategy, or political and economic development, there are no accidents: everything a culture produces is equally a symbol of that culture."[7] Cities don't just reflect the goals of city planners and the conscious intent of those who made them and live in them. They also make a bold statement about what we believe is important in life, what our idols are, even if we are not aware of them.

If we go to ancient cities in the Middle East, Far East, or Central America, we will find at their heart a palace or a temple. Often the palace and temple are the same thing, since many ancient civilizations treated rulers as divine. From the Egyptian Pharaoh to the Aztec Emperor these men were worshiped as the official gods.

If we look at the heart of medieval European cities, we find in them great cathedrals and churches symbolizing the fact that God (or perhaps the Church) was at the center of human life.

If we look at western cities, developed in the seventeenth and eighteenth centuries, we will find political structures—palaces, legislatures, and parliaments—at the center. This was the period when political authority began ascendancy in the west, and the state began to claim that it was the center of human life.

And what do we find if we look at the heart of our modern cities? Usually there are glass towers owned by banks or major corporations. These buildings also symbolize what lies close to the heart of these cities and close to the heart of too many of our lives—making money.

Obviously cities are much too complex to be completely understood by a single, simple scheme. They grow up over the ages as many succeeding idols hold sway. Hence, they always have many layers, including spiritual layers, built into them. Nevertheless, beyond all this complexity and variation, we can still see that the structures of our cities, towns, and suburbs themselves symbolize the deepest commitments of our life. Worship of idols or of the true God involves not just some small corner of human life, but it molds our living places and our very civilizations. A city is worship built large.

IDOLS OR DE-IDOLIZATION?

Indonesians love their roads and make good use of them. They're very useful for children to play in, for laying out crops to dry, for chickens and cows to wander around on, and often they are simply good places to sit down and have a chat. What those roads are less useful for, at least apart from the tollways in the larger cities, is getting from one place to another.

I had ample time to reflect on this as we struggled through the maze of alleys in Southern Jogjakarta, trying to find Edhy's place. He had moved a couple of times since our last visit, and it was some work tracking him down. Luckily the locals were friendly and helpful and often came along for the ride to make sure that we went to the right place. Finally we pulled up alongside a house with people carefully carving and painting on the porch. Since it had been five years since our last and only visit, I didn't think he'd remember me. But as I stepped into the front hall, a cheerful voice said, "Hey! Paul Marshall!"

Edhy not only has a great family, but he is also a great craftsman. He produces many things, but my favorites are his wayan kulit, *the famed Indonesian "shadow puppets." He works assiduously to make* them for performances at the Kraton (palace). Buffalo hide is carefully pressed and stretched, then intricately carved into the shape of the character. The carving is often so fine that the details of hair and feathers and clothing resemble filigree even in the tough leather. Next the puppets are painted; the finest detailing is done with a single hair. Finally, the puppet is carefully mounted on a stem of polished horn, and delicate horn rods are attached to the arms so the puppet can move.

I spent most of the day there, eating a late breakfast and watching and discussing the puppet carving.

The art of the wayan kulit is derived from Hinduism; the usual performances are epic Hindu myths and tales, many hours or even days long. Since many of the puppets appear to western eyes as strange, ferocious, and even demonic, I wondered how that art form had been contained and developed in what was now predominately a Muslim country.

At some point, I asked Edhy what his religion was. He replied with a smile, "Catholic."

I asked him if he had been brought up Catholic, and he said, "No, my parents are Muslims."

When I asked him why he became a Catholic, he replied with an even broader smile, "My wife told me to."

I asked him why she did that, and he replied with the biggest smile of all, "Catholics can only have one wife."

The conversation then returned to the puppets. I was curious to ascertain whether there were magical or occultic aspects to them. Not usually, he replied. And yet, he said that he fasts before making puppets to represent some of the evil characters. Most puppets represent characters of great memory and are symbols of courage or perseverance or intelligence: they are a delight to *make. But he is careful with the evil ones. Even so, the puppets had lost any directly spiritual significance and had simply become elements of great drama. So, to my mind, the greatest drama was unfolding in the puppet shop: a Catholic making Hindu-derived puppets for a cultural performance in a Muslim country. Idols were being tamed.*

In talks with Christian native peoples in Canada, we discussed their concerns about how much to incorporate traditional native spiritual practices into their Christian worship. What is inherently idolatrous, and what can be incorporated into true worship? These are not easy questions, and natives sometimes have differences among themselves. However, all agreed that if we are spiritually discerning, we can wisely make use of the great cultural skill and energy that have shaped these practices.

The Celtic crosses of Ireland are a good example. These crosses include a circle at the center, at the crux. The circle represented the sun, the chief symbol of the religion that the earliest Celtic Christians had slowly replaced. Was such a cross a deliberate compromise or even a thoughtless "watering down" of Christianity by an alien religion? Or did these crosses symbolize the triumph of cross over sun? Or did the Celtic Christians decide to honor the sun because it gives heat and light to each and every one of us and (though it is not divine) is ours as a gift from God himself? I think it is the last of these.

When we meet with Christians from other cultures, we westerners are sometimes far more critical of *their* attempts to "Christianize" their cultural heritage than we are of our *own* efforts. For example, on the anniversary of our Lord's birth, most western Christian homes are decorated with a large pagan symbol, a

Christmas tree. We also engage in rites such as gift giving that do not have a clear biblical precedent. Are we wrong to do so? I don't think so. The idolatrous associations of these practices have been stripped away by their incorporation into Christian traditions. On the other hand, in our commercial culture, the practice of gift giving may once again become idolatrous, as the focus of the holiday shifts from the birth of Christ to the exchange of presents.

But these dangers can be overcome. Just as it is the misplaced trust that we put in something, rather than the thing itself, that makes it an idol, so our using something without deifying it can be a work of de-idolization. This is how Paul dealt with meat offered to idols (1 Cor. 10:23–33). Idolatry is not a one-way process. Just as things can be made into idols, they can also be restored to their rightful place, becoming once more another of God's good gifts.

PLACING OUR IDOLS ON THE ALTAR

If we do not worship God, if we fall prey to idols, anything good in our lives can become a source of evil. Without genuine worship, our concerns with work and rest, play and politics, engineering and imagination, sex and sobriety will fall apart.

True worship must always be at the center of our lives. When we worship God, we are not so much going beyond the world as going into its heart. It is the core of our existence, the core of the creation itself, for everything was created in him, through him, and for him, and in him all things hold together (Col. 1:16–18).

Conversely, if our lives are not rooted and centered in worshiping God then we lay ourselves open to idols. The good things of the world will no longer be simply good things but will slowly move into and fill the emptiness at the heart of our lives. We will start to worship these good things or at least give them too much significance. As they begin to become separated from our faith, they will turn to evil. Even the greatest gifts will cause destruction if they are not subordinate to the gospel. The great Christian writer G. K. Chesterton observes that it is usually the good things that cause the greatest damage if they are divorced from God.

> *When a religious scheme is shattered it is not merely the vices that are let loose. The vices are, indeed, let loose, and they wander and do damage. But the virtues are let loose also, and the virtues wander more wildly, and the virtues do more terrible damage. The modern world is full of the old Christian virtues gone mad. The virtues have gone mad because they have been isolated from each other and are wandering alone. Thus some scientists care for truth; and their truth is pitiless. Thus some humanitarians only care for pity; and their pity (I am sorry to say) is often untruthful . . . what we suffer from is humility in the wrong place. Modesty has moved from the organ of ambition. Modesty has settled upon the organ of conviction, where it was never meant to be. A man was meant to be doubtful about himself, but undoubting about the truth; and this has been exactly reversed.*[8]

fourteen

E NLIGHTENED EVANGELISM

It was late evening in Minsk and, along with thousands of others, we walked up toward the Orthodox cathedral on the brow of the hill. It was Saturday night—Easter night—and we were gathering to celebrate Jesus' resurrection. Since Orthodox churches celebrate Easter on a different day from most Protestants, a group of us evangelicals gladly accepted the invitation to join in their worship.

The people from the Salvation Army and the independent gospel churches, the Presbyterians, the Baptists, and Pentecostals gathered in an upper room in the church building. There we had a luxury most of the worshipers did not—we could participate in the worship inside and also sense and see the crowds outside. The church only held about five hundred people, but ten thousand thronged outside, waiting in the cold night air around the entrance. Members of the Belarussian armed forces were gathered to hold the crowds back.

Only a couple of years before, troops had gathered there as well, in the same place at the same time, but then their job had been to drive the young people away. "This is church. It's only for old people. Go away!" Now the pressing crowd, both young and old, required soldiers, not for repression, but simply for order.

I sat next to the choir, their haunting cadences filling both the cathedral and the night air. At midnight, the Metropolitan (the Archbishop) led the clergy and those fortunate enough to be inside the cathedral out through the entrance and proclaimed triumphantly, "He is risen!"

The crowd, ourselves among them, called back, "He is risen indeed!"

The crowd bowed; we bowed; the soldiers bowed. And we rejoiced in the presence of our risen Lord among us. We marched around outside the church, proclaiming his resurrection. The worship continued into the small hours of the morning.

For most of the young people outside, many of them teenagers, the experience was new and strange, but they stayed to the end. Here, in a decaying remnant of the former Soviet Union, amidst buildings and roads in bleak disrepair, and amidst confusion, uncertainty, and growing poverty, these people had come together to witness a Light shining in the cold darkness. I do not know how many of them understood what was happening. They simply had an awareness that in that gray world, here was something that reached beyond their day-to-day existence and touched them with a glimpse of eternity.

As the night drew to an end, those who held lighted candles lit the candles of their neighbors. Those neighbors, in turn, lit the candles of their neighbors. The passage of flickering light continued through the crowd outside, till each soul held a light, shielded protectively against the night wind. These lights symbolized the *light of the one whose resurrection we celebrated. Then, carefully guarding the candles, we dispersed down the hill, along the quiet streets, and past shuttered homes into our own dwellings. There, we were to place the candles until, eventually together, we could testify to the light that had illuminated us.*

In every direction throughout the city, the lights went forth, gradually spreading out as they reached the byways and the alleys. Often they would disappear for a time as buildings blocked the light. Sometimes, we could see a soft, warm glow through a window, as a candle was placed in the midst of the home. Something of the Light of Jesus' resurrection had been placed in the hearts and homes of that grim city.

There in Minsk, before the eyes of the slowly awakening city, a picture was portrayed of our calling to share the Light of Christ. Evangelism involves showing forth the light of the gospel and the promise of the resurrection throughout the dark places of human life. It is placing the light of Christ in the center of human life.

We evangelicals have certain standard categories that are used to classify churches: "conservative," "liberal," or "Catholic." However, the Orthodox are something else again. Most evangelicals know little about them. It's true that all too often, Orthodox churches can succumb to a formal and ritualistic faith. But they also have strengths that we do not, and they have much to teach us. Frequently, they are weak on evangelism. But they also stress the presence of the risen Christ among us in everyday life. And this is something we very much need to learn.

Francis of Assisi said this about evangelism: "Preach the gospel constantly and, if necessary, use words." Many of us know the words of the gospel message. But what language can we use that could render words unnecessary? Our authentic friendships, quality of work, pleasurable company, personal integrity, and creative courage can communicate a truth about our lives. And above all else, our love for one another, for all people everywhere, and for all creation will speak eloquently of new life in Christ. "By this all men will know that you are my disciples, if you love one another" (John 13:25).

A HIGH AND HOLY CALLING

Through faith in Jesus Christ we have forgiveness of our sins and the sure hope of everlasting life with God: that is the core of the gospel. Evangelism is certainly also concerned with life after the resurrection, but it is also concerned with *this* life. It calls people to live a new life in Christ. This new life is service to Jesus Christ throughout the creation, in every aspect of human endeavor. We are called to a new life as preachers and artists, evangelists and truck drivers, deacons and scientists. We are called—and are calling other people—to a community that is alive and active in the world.

Sometimes it seems that our evangelism is about calling people to join an army that consists of nothing but recruiting officers—people who call other people to join the army. But people should be recruited into the army that is the Church in order to carry out a task *beyond* mere recruitment. Every Christian is called to be an evangelist, to share the gospel. But we are also called in the Scriptures to serve a new Master, to become part of a new humanity, a new race, a new nation. Proverbs says, "For from the heart flows the spring of life" (4:23, NJB). A new heart must lead to a new life. A new life expresses itself throughout every part of God's world.

Evangelism brings people into an expectation of the reconciliation of the world to God. It is an invitation to live in a new creation. As theologian Herman Bavinck wrote, "Christianity stands before the soul in its truth and holiness only when we . . . **glorify that Godlike** work wherein the Father reconciles his created but fallen world through the death of his Son, and recreates it by his Spirit into a Kingdom of God."

Jesus' words of farewell in the "Great Commission" echo the same theme. These words sometimes are read only as an exhortation to make individual converts. They certainly include that, but they also encompass far more.

"Then Jesus came to them and said, 'All authority in heaven and on earth has been given to me. Therefore go and make disciples of all nations, baptizing them in the name of the Father and of the Son and of the Holy Spirit, and teaching them to obey everything I have commanded you. And surely I am with you always, to the very end of the age.'" (Matt. 28:18–20).

We can be sure of this commission's success, because Jesus tells us he has authority not only in heaven but on earth as well. And because Jesus has authority over the nations, then the disciples are called to teach the nations to observe *all* he has commanded. The Great Commission itself includes our tasks in the world. The Great Commission is a calling creation-wide and creation-deep: *it calls the nations to obey God.*

When men and women turn to Jesus Christ in real, concrete repentance from sin and, by grace through faith, are restored in

God's favor, they are called to begin to live out the healing and restoration of Christ's redemption, taking up their Christian responsibility for the direction of human life and culture. Evangelism is, in a way, the recruiting process for this life whereby people are called out for service to God's kingdom. Evangelism calls people to repentance and to love for God. We are called to a new life of service to our neighbors. This is the Christian life.

A COMPELLING WAY OF LIFE

When we engage in sculpture or auto repair, politics or child rearing, farming or baseball, our *first* intention is not to win people to Jesus Christ. Instead we do these things because they are good, helpful, and of service and delight to people, because they can be rewarding and fun, and because God has called us to do them in faith.

If we try to make all our art, work, detective stories, or legislation simply a means to win others, we cause all sorts of problems. Our art will degenerate into propaganda. People will avoid talking to us at work, except to conduct essential business. Those around us will think that we don't take our writing seriously, or our job seriously, on its own account. Most important, they will assume that we don't take *them* seriously. This is why many non-Christians avoid evangelicals like the plague: they don't want to get grabbed, buttonholed, "shared" with, or otherwise commandeered.

But while our primary goal in the various areas of life should not be explicit evangelism, yet doing all our tasks wholeheartedly and well can be a tremendous aid to evangelism. If our daily actions do *not target* non-Christians, then non-Christians are more likely to be interested in them. If Christian faith produces good families, good businesses, good art, good books, and good politics, then people will notice, and they will be intrigued. In American society, where people think they know all they want to know about Christianity, this is especially important. As usual, C. S. Lewis said it well:

> *I believe that any Christian who is qualified to write a good pop-ular book on any science may do much more by that than by any directly apologetic [evangelistic] work. . . . We can make people (often) attend to the Christian point of view for half an hour or so; but the moment they have gone away from our lecture or laid down our article, they are plunged back into a world where the opposite position is taken for granted. . . . What we want is not more little books about Christianity, but more little books by Christians on other subjects—with their Christianity latent. You can see this most easily if you look at it the other way round. Our Faith is not very likely to be shaken by any book on Hinduism. But if whenever we read an elementary book on Geology, Botany, Politics, or Astronomy, we found that its implications were Hindu, that would shake us. It is not the books written in direct defense of Materialism that make the modern man a materialist; it is the materialistic assumptions in all the other books. In the same way, it is not books on Christianity that will really trouble him. But he would be troubled if, whenever he wanted a cheap popular introduction to some science, the best work on the market was always by a Christian.[1]*

GOOD GIFTS FROM GIFTED AUTHORS

One reason that C. S. Lewis was a great evangelist was that he wrote books of the very sort that he describes. Of course he also wrote great books of apologetics and evangelism. *Mere Christianity* is still one of the best books to give to non-Christians (provided they are interested). His book on evil, *The Problem of Pain*, or his spiritual autobiography, *Surprised by Joy*, which describes his own conversion, are classics for dealing with the many questions people have about the gospel. But these are not the books by Lewis that most non-Christians read. They read, or their children read, *The Chronicles of Narnia*.

The Narnia books contain Christian imagery, such as the parallels between the lion Aslan and Jesus. But Lewis was emphatic that these books were not disguised tracts, attempting to "smuggle in" Christian truth. They were simply children's books, designed to delight children with awe and wonder and fear and hope, to open their hearts and minds to wonderful possibilities.

But, like Dostoevsky's novels, the books are deeply Christian in this sense: they deal with struggles between good and evil, hope and despair, forgiveness and hatred. These are not presented as disguised evangelism but simply because they are the fundamental core of all real human drama and struggle: they are the center of human life. And because they are so deeply Christian, they are excellent children's books.

Similarly, it is true that the Bible is "the greatest story ever told." The Bible is, of course, far more than a story. It is *the true story* about human life. *It is because it is true that it has such power*. Despite our society's layers of confusion and denial, which try to wall us off from the meaning of being human, it touches the deepest chords within us. Even people who have no use for Christianity or Judaism can find the Bible to be an overwhelmingly important book. Those same people are able to enjoy Lewis as a source of delight and a goad to honest questioning.

There are other Christian authors who are also widely read. One is J. R. R. Tolkien, especially his *Lord of the Rings* trilogy. Tolkien wasn't trying, any more than his friend Lewis was trying, to write explicitly Christian books. He was simply in love with myth and legend and fantasy. He wanted, in a welter of wonderful words, to create a kingdom of innocence and evil, bravery and corruption, a world of bewildering variety, offering redemption and hope-beyond-hopelessness. Most people who read Tolkien do not know of his devout Catholic faith; they merely love what he created. The university students of my generation were obsessed with Tolkien—his books were all over campus. Even today this remains the case in many parts of the world.

Both Lewis and Tolkien wrote serious essays about the importance of fantasy-as-fantasy, a type of literature transcending any ulterior motive, evoking joy and wonder in people's lives. Thank God for that. Both men were also highly regarded professors of English literature; they had done their homework and they knew their stuff. But it is because they were simply interested in good stories, and able to write them artfully, that people continue to read them.

I have friends who first became open to Christianity when they found out that Tolkien and Lewis were Christians. They discovered this not from their books but because I told them (I wasn't trying to "smuggle it in," either; we were talking about faith and literature). The reason for my friends' openness was simple: if an author they loved was a Christian and, especially, if several authors they loved were Christians, then maybe Christianity was something they should consider more seriously. Neither Tolkien nor Lewis had tried to convert them; the authors had simply given them and their children a great gift. My friends wanted to know, in turn, what had moved the gift-givers.

There are others we could mention. Dorothy Sayers wrote explicitly Christian works such as *Creed or Chaos?* and *The Mind of the Maker*. They're good—in fact I've included several quotes from them. But most people read Sayers' detective stories, starring Lord Peter Wimsey. In fact one of the most remarkable things about the modern age is how many of the best current detective stories are written by Christians, and especially by Christian women.

Much of this is to do with the nature of the detective story, especially murder mysteries. They deal with life and death, good and evil, mystery and truth, and guilt and forgiveness. They are a genre of writing that the gospel opens up, and consequently many Christians are drawn to it and are good at it.

As illustrious as some literary Christians are, we do not have nearly the same examples in physics and economics, although Christian historians and philosophers are doing well. All these are a beginning, a sign that Christian culture, when done well and with diligence and integrity, will draw people to Jesus.

CHRISTIANITY IN THE MEDIA

There is another remarkable thing about these particular writers. They have *all* had movies made of their work, and not only big screen movies but also television shows. And it is not Christians who produce these films and videos. They are done by people who simply believe that these stories would be exciting on the screen. Let us get this straight: right now there are non-Christians who think it worthwhile to spend millions of dollars to bring the work of Christians to millions of people.

This is important for several reasons. One of them is that the screen—TV and movies—is *the* dominant means of communication in the modern world. One popular movie reaches more people than a million sermons. Because of this, the greatest "evangelist" in the 1990s is the director Steven Spielberg. I don't mean that he is a Christian evangelist but that he is a person who challenges and shapes what people believe about the ultimate issues of life.[2]

Spielberg is also an evangelist in this sense: when people sit down in offices, factories, homes, beaches, and bars, they talk about *E.T.* and *Schindler's List* and *Amistad* and *Saving Private Ryan,* and what these works say about life. Spielberg, more than any human being in America, sets the tone for how average Americans think about life's issues.

The screen—big or small—is what shapes our society, and Christians, with several notable and wonderful exceptions, are absent from the public screen. "Christian" TV is watched primarily by Christians. Few others care about it, if they are aware that it exists at all. Most of them hate it, in fact. How desperately we need careful, creative, thoughtful, courageous, and professional Christian screen works. YES

So why aren't they around? There are many reasons. For one thing, there really are non-Christian biases in American culture today. Christians in Hollywood or on network TV learn to keep their heads down. There can be bigotry and prejudice. But this is *not* the most important reason. The most basic reason is this—the screen does not lend itself to clear, forthright messages. You can't successfully preach on TV or in film. Preaching usually makes for lousy entertainment: people turn it off. That is the nature of the medium.

That's not to say that the screen doesn't "preach." On the contrary, it preaches persistenly, unrelentingly, and persuasively. But its preaching is always allusive, suggestive, and alluring; it hints, it frames, and it touches. It does not come right out and state the case; it does not argue. It is like the poet, not the essayist; the hymn writer, not the preacher. The strength of its preaching lies in the fact that its message is subsumed in something else.

Meanwhile, most Christians want to be direct and up front. We want to drive the point home, to make it absolutely clear. We are impatient with the allusion, the gesture, the suggested, the latent. We want the straightforward sermon, not the implied question. We want the forthright point, not the nagging suggestion. So we tend to stay away from serious TV.

This means we cut ourselves out of the most dominant means of human communication in the twentieth century. The Apostle Paul must be rolling in his grave. As he traveled, he used the best means of communication available to him—talking and writing. He talked and quoted and argued and debated, not only in synagogues, but also in markets, city squares, anywhere. He followed the trade routes—where news was most likely to travel. He hit the major centers, where the opinion-formers lived. He was sophisticated in the ways of the world. He used the dominant media.

I hesitate to say this because it sounds trite. But a modern Paul would use TV and make movies. And he would have been smart in the way he did it. He wouldn't have been "used" simply as the human-interest story of the day. People would have taken notice. After all, he was always being thrown into prison for his preaching. That's why he had time to write letters. Paul would either have been on *Larry King Live*, or else he would have been kept off the air because he was too controversial. Or both.

SET OUR HEARTS ON FIRE

Our Christian life is evidenced by what we say, in the plans we implement, and in the goals we follow. But it is also revealed by our manner, our personal style, and our attitudes. Mike Starkey writes:

> *The messages being sent out by countless Christians today are redolent of a past age. These Christians show by their observations on contemporary dress that they are victims of a knee-jerk conservatism, with a framework for assessing dress which automatically condemns anything new and unfamiliar. They are sending out messages to a watching world that to become a Christian, in addition to accepting the creeds, one will also have to find a way of living in a culture that no longer exists for most people. Our moral judgments are part of our mission. We need to tread carefully; a furrowed brow aimed at a Doc Marten boot or nose-ring in a morning service will say far more about our understanding of the gospel than a hundred sermons on the free grace of God.*[3]

Another aspect of such Christians as Lewis, Tolkien, and Sayers is that they are interesting people. It doesn't even matter, first of all, whether you believe their faith is true. They are intriguing because they write beautifully, and because they are quick-witted and amusing. In short, they are the sorts of people you would want to have in your house and at your party. They are stimulating, funny, and unpredictable.

And this brings us to another point about evangelism. Many people find Christians dull. They really don't want to come to our church because they fear that they'll be bored out of their skulls. How have we managed to leave this impression? We, who are called to be followers of the least boring person who ever existed. Dorothy Sayers comments:

> *Somehow or other, and with the best intentions, we have shown the world the typical Christian in the likeness of a crashing and rather ill-natured bore—and this in the Name of one who assuredly never bored a soul in those thirty-three years during which He passed through this world like a flame.*[4]

And it is not just the person of Jesus, staggering though he is, that brings excitement to the gospel. The whole drama of redemption overturns every human conceit and limit. God made the world and loves it; God loves us and will forgive us and make us live forever. God became a human being and was born from inside the womb of a woman. He lived on earth and shared our joys and delights, our grief and pain. He literally died, literally rose again, and invites us to join him. No human mind could conceive such a life and person and drama and hope. However could we have made it pedestrian and dull? Again, Dorothy Sayers: "It is the dogma that is the drama—not beautiful phrases, nor comforting sentiments, nor vague aspirations to loving kindness and uplift, nor the promise of something nice after death—but the terrifying assertion that the same God who made the world lived in the world and passed through the grave and gate of death. Show that to the heathen, and they may not believe it; but at least they may realize that here is something that a man might be glad to believe."[5]

As we discussed various types of evangelism, a Pentecostal pastor grinned mischievously. Pressed to explain, he talked about his boyhood in a small town on the Canadian prairies. Near the town was a large Bible college, and each year the college freshmen had a required course in evangelism. Toward the end of the term, one of their course requirements was to actually engage in personal evangelism. And so, during that week of the semester, about 300 young evangelists emerged from the campus, eager to find people with whom they could "share the gospel."

The college was in the middle of flat, endless prairie grasslands, and the only people in the vicinity were the inhabitants of the local town. Consequently, the number of budding witnesses out-numbered the potential witnessees two to one.

The townsfolk had become used to this, since it happened every fall. It was a thing they expected, just as they expected the trees to change and the temperatures to fall. Some planned to get out of town that week, but a majority of the townsfolk stayed and took it in good grace. After all, most of them were already believers anyway.

Nonetheless, it could be difficult, for example, trying to go to the hardware store and having to run a gauntlet of evangelists. The evangelism students were always bright, cheerful, and polite.

They would strive earnestly to avoid giving offense to anybody. But most of the locals would sooner have been left alone so they could carry out their various errands in peace.

Some of the locals found it frustrating to have to keep insisting that they were believers. Others were equally annoyed at having to repeat that they'd heard it all before and right now they weren't interested, thank you very much. Still others found it quicker simply to go along with the program and pray—yet again—for God's forgiveness. It was faster that way, and then you could get on with your business.

With a smile, the pastor reported that some townspeople used to get converted up to half a dozen times on a single day.

fifteen

PATIENCE AND LONG-SUFFERING

The meeting room was a large grass hut. It had been built only a couple of days before, so the Sudanese government would not know in advance where it was and be able to bomb it. The location was secret, and the surrounding glade was dotted with guerrillas, usually discreetly hidden but ready to emerge and search the people who came.

Around the hut were large pits full of water, which strangely seemed to have been placed outside the meeting room entrances so that in the dark, you would fall in, as one man from Barcelona did. When we asked what the holes were for, we were told that originally they had been dug as bomb shelters, but then the rains had come early.

After receiving permission from their superiors, the men stationed at the surrounding anti-aircraft batteries proudly posed with their guns, their white teeth flashing brilliantly underneath the camouflaging trees. I wished them well, since I had no desire to escape from bombing by jumping into a muddy trench filled with fetid water that was already teeming with not-so-little crawling things.

Amidst the armed soldiers and people dressed in western suits or colorful African clothing passed bishops—both Episcopal and Catholic—distinguished by their purple vests but wearing the same flashing smiles. Another man sauntered amongst the crowd, clad in a sharp black three-piece suit, with broad sunglasses and a wide-brimmed hat. He appeared to be a throwback from the Harlem of the 1930s.

The air was often filled with laughter in the evening, and throughout the glades could be heard the sounds of earnest conversation and argument, and frequently of prayer and hymn singing.

The gathering had been organized by the Sudan People's Liberation Movement and the Sudan People's Liberation Army. It brought together representatives from relief agencies, "experts," and people from the southern part of Sudan. Many of these people, victimized by a genocidal war waged by the Sudanese government in Khartoum, had seen their villages destroyed, their crops burned, their altars machine-gunned, their relatives and friends killed, and their children taken into slavery. They were gathered now for a conference on "civil society," on how they could and should freely operate the parts of the country they now controlled.

I had been asked to speak to the conference on the subject of "The Structure of Civil Society"—a topic that seemed a million light-years from the reality of our surroundings. Near the back of the room were women and men from the Nuba Mountains in central Sudan. To get to the meeting, they had walked through a *war zone, territory occupied by marauding militias and roaming slave traders. Some of them had walked for seventy-two days to be at the conference. No doubt they would have to walk another seventy-two days to get back. They were the people who were often laughing at the back and singing in the evening. They were also the people who knew best about long-suffering.*

Jesus told the disciples that the kingdom of God had already come: "The kingdom of God does not come with your careful observation, nor will people say, 'Here it is,' or 'There it is,' because *the kingdom of God is within you*" (Luke 17:20–21).

"If I drive out demons by the Spirit of God, then *the kingdom of God has come upon you*" (Matt. 12:26–28).

"*The kingdom of God is near.* Repent and believe the good news!" (Mark 1:15).

"*You are not far from the kingdom of God*" (Mark 12:24).

"I tell you the truth, some who are standing here will *not taste death before they see the kingdom of God come with power*" (Mark 9:1).

The Bible says the kingdom of God is already here. We inhabit it day by day, and our service to God and to one another is part of the kingdom. We can already taste the fruits of God's grace, and his healing hand already touches the world.

But the Bible says that we also live in a reality that is in many ways unchanged. We still live in a world full of evil, sickness, and death. We still despair, we still doubt, we still sin. Much of what God has promised still lies ahead of us. Some days it seems a long, long way ahead of us. This is why we are a people who are called to live by promise. We look for that which has been promised but which is not yet present. This is why we are also a people who are called to live by hope, to be "certain of what we do not see" (Heb. 11:1). We are a people who are called to live by faith.

Though sin continues to thrive in the world, and though Jesus has not yet returned, our citizenship is still in heaven (Phil. 3:20). Like Abraham, we are sojourners who are looking for a city that is yet to come (Heb. 11:8–10), who are still waiting to enter into rest (Heb. 4:1–11).

But this is not the end of the story. When Paul says that our citizenship is in heaven, he does not say that our final *destination* is heaven, since he adds that it is from heaven that "we eagerly await our Savior . . . who, by the power that enables him to bring everything under his control, will transform our lowly bodies so that they will be like his glorious body . . . therefore . . . you should stand firm in the Lord" (Phil. 3:20–4:1).

Our hope, our joy, our expectation is *from* heaven; our resurrection, our renewal, our rejoicing will surely come from there. Who we are and how we live will be transformed. Therefore we yearn, we await, we are patient, and, above all, we are filled with hope. Help is coming.[1] Much of the help is not here as yet, however, and death, corruption, laziness, persecution, and torture are still with us. The wicked often win out. The righteous, the noble, the brave, the faithful still often live and die in an ongoing struggle with whatever affliction the world can impose upon them. Therefore we are a people who must live not only in hope but also in patience and in what the Bible calls "long-suffering"— suffering for, perhaps, a long time. We must, as the Scripture so often says, *wait on the Lord.*

PATIENCE AND THE KINGDOM

The letter to the Hebrews teaches us of faith and hope and so, as a result, urges us to "run with perseverance the race marked out for us" (Heb. 12:1). What type of race do people run with perseverance, with patience? A sprinter does not run with patience: he or she dashes out of the blocks, accelerates as fast as possible, and runs at full speed until the finish. There's no time for strategy, for pacing, for guarding one's strength. It's all over in ten seconds, in a burst of immediate, frantic, and exhilarating energy.

But this is not the type of race that is to mark our life. Our race is like the 1,500 meters, or, more likely, the marathon—long, grueling hours of sweat and agony. We have to be careful at the start because we don't want to burn out before the end and not finish the course. We judge carefully how much stamina is needed for each lap, each stretch. We pace ourselves so that at the end, whether minutes hence or hours hence, we will have used all the energy we possess in the wisest way. We run with discipline.

The Bible stresses that God is going to judge the world. But it also stresses that a major part of this judgment will take place in the future. Jesus told this parable:

> *The kingdom of heaven is like a man who sowed good seed in his field. But while everyone was sleeping, his enemy came and sowed weeds among the wheat, and went away. When the wheat sprouted and formed heads, then the weeds also appeared. The owner's servants came to him and said, "Sir, didn't you sow good*

seed in your field? Where then did the weeds come from?" "An enemy did this," he replied.

Matthew 13:24–28a

When the servants asked whether the weeds should be uprooted he answered,

"No . . . because while you are pulling the weeds, you may root up the wheat with them. Let both grow together until the harvest. At that time I will tell the harvesters: First collect the weeds and tie them in bundles to be burned; then gather the wheat and bring it into my barn."

Matthew 13:29–30

Jesus went on to explain that this referred to the future judgment:

"The one who sowed the good seed is the Son of Man. The field is the world, and the good seed stands for the sons of the kingdom. The weeds are the sons of the evil one, and the enemy who sows them is the devil. The harvest is the end of the age, and the harvesters are angels. As the weeds are pulled up and burned in the fire, so it will be at the end of the age. The Son of Man will send out his angels, and they will weed out of his kingdom everything that causes sin and all who do evil. They will throw them into the fiery furnace, where there will be weeping and gnashing of teeth. Then the righteous will shine like the sun in the kingdom of their Father. He who has ears, let him hear."

Matthew 13:36–43

In this age God lets good and evil co-exist, lest further damage be done. God is patient with the world, lest anything good be lost. And, if God is patient even with those who do evil, how much more are we called to exercise such patience. Many of the things promised are "not yet," and we can cause even greater suffering if we try to grasp hold of them now. There are good things that we cannot see now. There are also evil things that we cannot escape now.

Being patient in the face of sin doesn't mean we believe that sinful ways of life are good or that it doesn't matter what anyone does. It simply means that not all things can be fixed right now. We cannot right all wrongs; we cannot stop all evil; we cannot compel all to follow God's ways. We have to endure these things, often with long-suffering. We are not in a sprint; we are in a marathon, we have miles to go, and we will not quickly cross the finish line. We must run on in a world of intermingled healing and pain, good and evil.

OUR LONG-SUFFERING LORD

God not only allows people to live in disobedience to him, he also actively cares for them despite their disobedience. Jesus told us to love not only our friends but also our enemies, just like our Father does. "Love your enemies . . . that you may be children of your father who is in heaven; for he makes his sun to rise on the evil and on the good. And sends the rain on the just and on the unjust" (Matt. 5:45).

God doesn't simply put up with those who turn against him; he actively cares for and loves them day by day. The sun's rising is a sign of God's continuing love and care, and it rises on everyone. The rain is God's continuing gift, and it provides life to everyone, whether they are just or not. The creation is God's and he actively sustains it, loves it, and cares for it. It is only God's continual, caring love that makes it even possible to disobey him.

As we struggle to find a Christian way to live in our modern age, we must know that we will not be able to overcome all those things that we think are wrong. Sin continues to corrupt our world, destroy our lives, and frustrate our hopes. The wheat and the tares will go on growing together. Until Christ's return, sin must not only be strenuously fought but also painfully borne. We need to nurture not only the virtues of truth and confrontation but also of patience and long-suffering.

One additional reason for this patience is our own need for sanctification. It trains us and prepares us to live both with one another and in the new heavens and earth that God will bring about. As the Apostle Paul writes,

> *Therefore, since we have been justified through faith, we have peace with God through our Lord Jesus Christ, through whom we have gained access by faith into this grace in which we now stand. And we rejoice in the hope of the glory of God. Not only so, but we also rejoice in our sufferings, because we know that suffering produces perseverance; perseverance, character; and character, hope. And hope does not disappoint us, because God has poured out his love into our hearts by the Holy Spirit, whom he has given us.*
>
> Romans 5:1–5

And Paul emphasizes that this promise is not only for us. He again takes up the themes of patience and suffering later in the same letter:

Now if we are children, then we are heirs—heirs of God and co-heirs with Christ, if indeed we share in his sufferings in order that we may also share in his glory. I consider that our present suffer-ings are not worth comparing with the glory that will be revealed in us. The creation waits in eager expectation for the sons of God to be revealed. For the creation was subjected to frustration, not by its own choice, but by the will of the one who subjected it, in hope that the creation itself will be liberated from its bondage.

Romans 8:17–21

The creation itself is suffering and waiting, with us and for us.

The biblical picture of a "new heaven and a new earth" should fill us with hope and expectation. But it should not cause us to be arrogant or overconfident in our service. It is true that our task spans the entire creation. It is true that we will see new heavens and a new earth. It is true that in Jesus Christ the power of sin has already been overcome. He said: "Be of good cheer, I have over-come the world" (John 16:33). But the completion of this great redemption awaits his return. "Be of good cheer," Jesus said to the disciples, but also "In the world you have tribulation." He warned them, "Think not that I am come to send peace on earth: I came not to send peace, but a sword" (Matt. 10:34).

We do not live now in a time of perfection and wholeness, for the kingdom of God has not yet come in completeness. But nei-ther do we live in a time exclusively of pain and failure, for the kingdom of God is already here. We live in the time before the final winnowing, the time when the wheat and the tares will continue to grow together. We cannot and should not expect any immediate final victory over evil. But we can expect what Francis Schaeffer has called "substantial healing"—real changes and real fruits of peace and love. We can still make a difference, patiently.

You suffered throughout your life, O Lord Jesus Christ, that I might be saved. And yet, even now, you continue to bear with me, as I stumble upon the path and constantly go astray. As often as I become impatient and wish to abandon your way, you encourage me and stretch forth your helping hand. Each day I increase your burden; yet while I am impatient your patience is infinite.[2]

sixteen

THE NEW CREATION

Brother Felipe died just before we returned to Culion. He was old, although nobody knew quite how old. When some sixty or seventy years before his family had discovered his leprosy, he'd been cursed with the same fate that befell such Filipino children. He was immediately removed from his home and left in a "leper colony." He didn't know at what age this had happened him; only that it was before he was five. He didn't know who his family was or where he had come from. He grew up among other lepers in the outpost to which they, too, had been assigned. There he had found peace in Jesus Christ and later had become an elder and pillar of the small Protestant church.

Brother Felipe had possessed deep tranquillity, calm assurance, and a ready if somewhat crooked smile.

Brother Felipe's friends and his children delayed the funeral for as long as they could in the hope that other members of his family could come, particularly his daughter, who had set off for Japan. However, after a couple of days, he simply had to be buried. The island is hot and muggy. Vegetation grows fast, and bodies decay even faster.

Brother Felipe's family asked me if I would preach at his funeral. This would be thought a great honor—to have a foreigner, a westerner, a professor, even, to speak at his funeral. Not many such come that way.

As for me, I wanted to run as far away as I could to hide the fact that, compared to these people, I knew nothing about faith, about peace, about joy, or about hope. I couldn't imagine what I could possibly say at a funeral in a Filipino leprosarium. But to have declined would have added insult to deep pain, so I said yes.

I couldn't sleep the night before the funeral. It was hot and humid. Dogs howled, lizards scuttled up the walls, insects hummed. I couldn't shake the feeling that the mosquito net had holes in it. But the outside distractions were a minor part of it. I would have slept no better if I had been spending the night at the Ritz. It was what was inside that made me want to slink away, afraid of revealing my ignorance and trivial faith.

Since I couldn't sleep and didn't know what I would say, I went shortly before sunrise to the little hall where Brother Felipe's body lay in state. The simple coffin was painted black, and above his face there was, as was customary, a thin glass panel so one could look in and see him. I was afraid to do this, since the body of this elderly leper had lain in tropical heat for two days. But I did—alone in the morning light. I was relieved to see that his eyes were closed and his face was serene.

I sat in front of the coffin and looked around for inspiration, still half-contemplating whether to bolt on the morning boat. I glanced at the communion table behind the coffin, to the profu-

sion of flowers displayed upon it. They had been plucked from the shrubs and the bushes all around—such common flowers that I almost hadn't noticed them. But they were beautiful, and they festooned the church in brilliant tactile reds and pinks and yellows and blues and greens. They seemed still to be growing, even though they had been cut away from living plants.

I noticed, too, that upon the coffin, against the flat black surface, other flowers had been painted in simple white strokes. They were gathered round the edges, and as I looked back on the top of the coffin, near the glass panel, I realized that yet more flowers were painted there.

"Why flowers?" I wondered.

Nearly everywhere there are flowers. Flowers are always present at Christian funerals back home. Flowers are used at funerals in Russia and Africa, and flowers were here. Why? Because flowers represent beauty and new life. Solomon in all his glory cannot be compared to one of them. Yet they spring up easily and they die. They are cast back into the earth. And then they grow again. Flowers are signs of new life and hope. And there, at the front of that simple room, lay Brother Felipe, adorned and surrounded with flowers.

During that early morning vigil, God spoke to me about new life and hope, of how the former things had passed away and the new things had begun. And so I was able to speak that morning of how Brother Felipe was, by God's grace, like those flowers. I spoke of the hidden beauty of his soul, of his faith, of his tenderness. Now he had died, and we had marked his death with flowers and with beauty because we know that he will rise again. We know that the beauty of his soul will once again shine. And not only his soul, but also his body. When you have leprosy, the promise of a new body has a meaning few others can grasp. Brother Felipe died in peace, content in the full promise of a new life in a new body in a new heaven and earth.

I did not say to that funeral gathering that I had only come to learn something of the meaning of the resurrection in those dawn hours; those who heard me already knew its meaning. But I had learned, once more, that the crucial lessons of life do not come from books or from study; they come from the life of the faithful in suffering, rejoicing, living, and dying. There, in human flesh, is lived out Paul's promise, "For I am convinced that neither death nor life, neither angels nor demons, neither the present nor the future, nor any powers, neither height nor depth, nor anything else in all creation, will be able to separate us from the love of God that is in Christ Jesus our Lord" (Rom. 8:38–39).

The Bible speaks to us of the resurrection *of the body*. Job declared, "I know that my redeemer lives" and that "in my flesh I will see God" (Job 19:25, 26). The words of the Apostle's Creed, the universal creed of the Christian church, are repeated in most churches each Sunday—"I believe in the resurrection of the body and the life everlasting." Jesus rose again from the dead in the body.

Despite the fact that we say those words with our lips, often they do not penetrate our hearts and minds. Still hovering in our consciousness is the thought that our future will really be disembodied. We somehow imagine that God made a mistake, that he really intended for us to be some kind of pure spirit. Two-thirds of Americans believe that they will not have bodies after the resurrection.[1]

A CLOSER LOOK AT THE
RESURRECTION OF THE BODY

We know that after Jesus rose from the dead, he walked on the earth. He broke bread with the disciples (Luke 24:30), he cooked (John 21:9), and he ate fish with them (Luke 24:41–43). When the disciples were troubled, he asked them, "Why are you troubled and why do doubts rise in your minds? Look at my hands and my feet. It is I myself. Touch me and see; a ghost does not have flesh and bones, as you see I have" (Luke 24:38–39).

When Thomas doubted, Jesus reaffirmed his presence in the body: "Put your finger here; see my hands. Reach out your hand and put it in my side. Stop doubting and believe" (John 20:27).

Certainly there were things different about the resurrected Jesus. For example, he appeared among the disciples even though the doors were locked (John 20:19; see also 1 Cor. 15:35–58). But, whatever the differences, the similarities to his life before his death were profound. He was no ghost. He was no disembodied spirit. He was flesh and bones; he walked, he cooked, and he ate. Why should we imagine that we will be any less substantial? John Updike wrote:

> *Make no mistake: if He rose at all*
> *It was as His body;*
> *If the cells' dissolution did not reverse, the molecules reknit,*
> *the amino acids rekindle,*
> *the Church will fall.*

It was not as the flowers,
Each soft spring recurrent;
It was not as His Spirit in the mouths and fuddled eyes of the
eleven apostles;
It was as His flesh: ours.

The same hinged thumbs and toes,
The same valved heart
That—pierced—died, withered, paused, and then regathered
Out of enduring Might
New strength to enclose.

Let us not mock God with metaphor,
Analogy, sidestepping, transcendence,
Making of the event a parable, a sign painted in the faded
Credulity of earlier ages:
Let us walk through the door.

The stone is rolled back, not papier-mâché
not a stone in a quarry
but the vast rock of materiality that in the slow grinding of
time will eclipse for each of us
the wide light of day.[2]

PURIFIED LIKE FINEST GOLD

Our bodies will not be forever lost, nor will the earth be cast
away. Instead, our bodies will be renewed, just as our souls will
be renewed. Sometimes we are misled because we don't fully

understand Peter's statement that the world is being reserved for fire (2 Pet. 3:7).

Peter's letter does not contradict the view that the world will be preserved. In fact, that is what he teaches. When he writes that "the present heavens and earth are reserved for fire, being kept for the day of judgment," he ends the sentence by referring to the "destruction of ungodly men" (2 Pet. 3:7). He is writing about the fire of judgment that destroys the sinful and the wrong, not the fire of destruction that destroys the creation itself.[3]

To drive the point home, Peter draws an explicit parallel with the time of Noah when, "By these waters also the world of that time was deluged and destroyed." But we know from Genesis that the world did not cease to exist after the flood. The "world" that was destroyed was not the "world" of the creation itself but the "world" of sinful people. The sinful world—the conspiracy of evil against God—was destroyed. But Noah and his family and the animals and the birds were rescued in order to begin life again. The flood was a time of purification. The fire of judgment will be similar.

Peter goes on: "The heavens will disappear with a roar, the elements will be destroyed by fire, and the earth and everything in it will be laid bare" (2 Pet. 3:10). The imagery here is of the refiner's fire (compare with Mal. 3:2–4). It is the imagery of a world *renewed* (*kainos*). When we refine metal, we take the impure ore and cast it into a blast furnace, where soil, impure elements, and unwanted minerals are burned off in the incandescent heat. At the end the pure metal—the gold, the silver—is poured forth and appears in shimmering, luminous beauty. This is the imagery that suffuses Peter's description of the judgment.

This picture is much like the parable of the wheat and the tares to which we referred earlier. The good grain will be harvested, the weeds cast aside and burned (Matt. 13:24–30). John the Baptist prophesied the coming of Jesus with the same expectation: "His winnowing fork is in his hand, and he will clear his threshing floor, gathering his wheat into the barn and burning up the chaff with unquenchable fire" (Matt. 3:12). This is why the New International and other recent Bible translations have replaced the older King James depiction that "the earth also and the works that are therein shall be burned up," with the words, "the earth and everything in it will be *laid bare* [or found]" (2 Pet. 3:10). By destroying the evil and purifying the good, God's refining fire of judgment will expose things as they really are. When judgment is passed, the earth will once more be found.

MAKING WAY FOR THE NEW HEAVENS

Nor is the judgment directed only at the earth, but at the heavens also. From somewhere we seem to have acquired the idea that only the earth has been touched by sin, and only the earth stands under judgment. Certainly it is true that the Bible does not tell us very much about heaven, just as it does not tell us very much about what the new heavens and the new earth will be like. And what the Bible does say is often in very poetic language. God seems most concerned that we know it will be glorious, that we will live with him, and that Jesus will be in our midst. But what we do know indicates that sin has affected heaven as well as earth. The devil appears to be a fallen angel, cast out from heaven (Isa. 14:12–15; Job 1:6, 2:1).

Jesus himself speaks of seeing "Satan fall like lightning from heaven" (Luke 10:17–18).

Peter certainly teaches about the judgment of heaven as well as earth. He writes that "the present heavens and earth are reserved for fire, being kept for the day of judgment"(v. 7); "the heavens will disappear with a roar" (v. 10); and of "the destruction of the heavens by fire" (v. 12). That is why we do not look for the end of the earth and its replacement by heaven, but rather we look "forward to a new heaven and a new earth, the home of righteousness" (v. 13).

The biblical imagery is not of the replacement of the earth by heaven, but one of a new heaven and earth that are unified and where Jesus will be in the midst of the earth. The angel tells John of "the new Jerusalem, which is coming down out of heaven" (Rev. 3:12). In the closing acts of Scripture, portrayed in the book of Revelation, John writes,

> *Then I saw a new heaven and a new earth, for the first heaven and the first earth had passed away, and there was no longer any sea. I saw the Holy City, the new Jerusalem, coming down out of heaven from God, prepared as a bride beautifully dressed for her husband. And I heard a loud voice from the throne saying, "Now the dwelling of God is with men, and he will live with them. They will be his people, and God himself will be with them and be their God. He will wipe every tear from their eyes. There will be no more death or mourning or crying or pain, for the old order of things has passed away. . . ."*
>
> *And he carried me away in the Spirit to a mountain great and high, and showed me the Holy City, Jerusalem, coming down out of heaven from God.*

Revelation 21:1–4, 10

The present world faces not the destructive fire of annihilation but the purifying fire of judgment. Those things that are praiseworthy, both the gifts that God has given to us and the works that we have created, will find their place in the new creation: all good is everlasting. The Bible promises us a new heaven and a new earth, and in the center of the earth lies the Holy City, the New Jerusalem. In the center of the city is Jesus Christ in whom everything in heaven and earth finds its ultimate fulfillment. Here is a world healed, restored, and re-centered.

GOD'S CITY, NOT GOD'S GARDEN

As John describes the culmination of redemption, the reconciliation of God with his people, the fruition of life upon earth, he sees no longer a garden, as in Eden at the beginning, but a city, the creation of human culture. Instead of a city conceived in human pride, it is a city given as a gift of God. What had been begun in sin by Cain and at Babel is now portrayed in its perfection.

It is true that this is *God's* city, but clearly it is God's *city*, not God's garden. John also sees the bride, not naked, as with Adam and Eve in Eden, but now clothed, "richly adorned for her husband." Adam and Eve had clothed themselves with fig leaves because of shame resulting from their sin. Even then God had reached out to them by providing them with better clothing (Gen. 3:21). Now God is finishing and perfecting this clothing; the appearance of the bride shows humanity in clothing that is richly prepared, exquisite enough to be presented to Jesus Christ.

The prophecies of the reign of the Messiah also emphasize his earthly rule; the new heaven and the new earth will even include work and rest. Isaiah prophesies that with the reign of the Messiah:

> *They will build houses and dwell in them; they will plant vineyards and eat their fruit. No longer will they build houses and others live in them, or plant and others eat. For as the days of a tree, so will be the days of my people; my chosen ones will long enjoy the works of their hands.*

Isaiah 65:21–22

In the reign of Jesus upon earth, we will not cease to work, since this is our created nature. Rather, work will be freed from the pain of sin and will, at last, become what God intended from the beginning. Instead of toiling with little reward, we will enjoy the fruits of our labors; we will eat the fruits of our own vineyards and peacefully delight in what we have produced.

The theme of the riches of the earth entering the City of God is repeated throughout Scripture. Isaiah prophesies the glory of Zion that is to come:

> *Nations will come to your light,*
> *and kings to the brightness of your dawn.*
> *Lift up your eyes and look about you:*
> *All assemble and come to you;*
> *your sons come from afar,*
> *and your daughters are carried on the arm.*
> *Then you will look and be radiant,*
> *your heart will throb and swell with joy;*
> *the wealth on the seas will be brought to you,*

to you the riches of the nations will come.
Herds of camels will cover your land,
young camels of Midian and Ephah.
And all from Sheba will come,
bearing gold and incense
and proclaiming the praise of the LORD.
All Kedar's flocks will be gathered to you,
the rams of Nebaioth will serve you;
they will be accepted as offerings on my altar,
and I will adorn my glorious temple.
Who are these that fly along like clouds,
like doves to their nests?
Surely the islands look to me;
in the lead are the ships of Tarshish,
bringing your sons from afar, with their silver and gold,
to the honor of the LORD your God, the Holy One of Israel,
for he has endowed you with splendor. . . .
Your gates will always stand open,
they will never be shut, day or night,
so that men may bring you the wealth of the nations—
their kings led in triumphal procession. . . .
The glory of Lebanon will come to you,
the pine, the fir and the cypress together,
to adorn the place of my sanctuary;
and I will glorify the place of my feet.
The sons of your oppressors will come bowing before you;
all who despise you will bow down at your feet
and will call you the City of the LORD,
Zion of the Holy One of Israel.

Isaiah 60:1–14

BEATING SWORDS INTO PLOWSHARES

Zion, the Holy City, is also the city of the earth's treasures. The riches of the nations will be there; the kings of the earth will be there, too. When we read the famous words (now engraved on the United Nations building in New York) "they will beat their swords into ploughshares and their spears into pruning hooks" (Mic. 4:35), we learn more about what God promises. The prophet Micah not only prophesies the destruction of implements for war, and the reign of the Prince of Peace, but he also foretells the (new) creation of implements for service. Whatever it is we are to do when Jesus reigns, apparently we will need plows and pruning hooks to accomplish our tasks.[4]

AND THE WORKS OF OUR HEARTS WILL BE THERE

Human stewardship of the earth is perfected at the coming of Christ. John also sees that the kings of the earth will not only come into the city but will also bring their splendor into it (Rev. 21:24). The flow of human history, the outworking of God's act of creation, continues and is taken up in the renewed heavens and earth.

Our works, here and now, are not all transitory. The good that we have done will not simply disappear and be forgotten. This world is not a passing and futile phase; it will be taken up in God's new world. Our good buildings, our great inventions, our acts of healing, our best writings, our creative art, our finest clothes, our greatest treasures will not simply pass away. If they represent the finest works of God's image-bearers, they will adorn the world to come.

Certainly, many of the things we do will be too marked by sin and will be rejected and burned up. But our actions upon God's earth are not futile; we are not whiling away the hours for something that will ultimately be destroyed at the last day. The good will endure forever. In Isaiah's closing prophecy his vision leaps ahead to see the future of Israel in terms of God's ultimate plans and he weaves together all of these themes:

> *See, the LORD is coming with fire,*
> *and his chariots are like a whirlwind;*
> *he will bring down his anger with fury,*
> *and his rebuke with flames of fire.*
> *For with fire and with his sword the LORD*
> *will execute judgment upon all men,*
> *and many will be those slain by the LORD. . . .*
> *"And I . . . am about to come and gather all nations and tongues,*
> *and they will come and see my glory. . . .*
> *They will proclaim my glory among the nations.*
> *And they will bring all your brothers, from all the nations,*
> *to my holy mountain in Jerusalem as an offering to the LORD*
> *—on horses, in chariots and wagons, and on mules and camels,"*
> *says the LORD.*
> *"They will bring them, as the Israelites bring their grain offerings,*
> *to the temple of the LORD in ceremonially clean vessels.*
> *As the new heavens and the new earth that I make will endure*
> *before me," declares the LORD.*
>
> Isaiah 66:15, 16, 18, 19, 20, 22

For all who long for a genuine "happy ending" to life's story, there is reason for hope. That which is good and just will be purified. That which is evil and unjust will be destroyed when "the kingdom of the world has become the kingdom of our Lord and of his Christ . . . and he will reign for ever and ever" (Rev. 11:5).

seventeen

B̲ETWEEN̲
TIMES̲

Christians are African women who rise at dawn to greet the rising sun in a wailing chant of thanks to God. They are Indian untouchables clearing up excrement from the streets. They are slaves in Sudanese markets. They are Chinese peasants flip-flopping by rice fields or pedaling bicycles through Shanghai. They are Mexican tribal people, driven from their ancestral homes. They are Filipina maids, misused throughout the world. They are Russian Orthodox priests, hit by cars which mysteriously careen onto the sidewalk. They are Arab women who have been raped and had acid poured on them to remove distinguishing Christian marks. And, overwhelmingly, they are people who, given a moment's time, space, and freedom, live life with joy, enthusiasm, and gratitude.[1]

This world is our home: we are made to live here. It has been devastated by sin, but God plans to put it right. Hence, we look forward with joy to newly restored bodies and to living in a newly restored heaven and earth. We can love this world because it is

God's, and it will be healed, becoming at last what God intended from the beginning. We are not merely passing through this world and this life. We are shaping the building blocks of eternity.

In this light, I've talked about life, and experiencing life, and enjoying life, and being immersed in life. I've talked about the wonder and the joy of God's world. I've talked about loving creation and throwing ourselves fully and joyfully into the tasks and opportunities that lie before us, that greet us with each new day. But, sometimes, this can sound like a false promise, since each of us struggles with problems in our jobs, our marriages, our families, our neighborhoods, and the daily feeling of being overwhelmed. We may face poverty, disability, disease, pain, imprisonment, and death.

JOY IN THE MIDST OF PAIN

Against the backdrop of a gray Monday, promises of hope in a renewed world can seem inflated, even cavalier. None of our problems have gone away or even grown smaller. However, I do not say these things from out of my own narrow experience. My confidence in these truths stems from the lives of people whose trials and sufferings most of us cannot even begin to imagine. In a previous book, *Their Blood Cries Out*, I wrote about the persecution of Christians throughout the world, millions of whom have suffered and died simply because they named the name of Jesus Christ. Their lives call out to us. Their lives provide a testimony to what new hope and new life in God's world brings. They show us that in the midst of questions, of worries, of fears, of frustrations, of disappointments, of failures, and even more, of pain, imprisonment, and death, God's grace illumines our hearts and shows us that we can live beyond them all.

These women, men, and children show us that, as Jesus said, "My grace is sufficient for you" (2 Cor. 12:9). Our lives are not to be hoarded and protected and spent in miserly fashion as the days go by. Our lives are to be lived, to be cast fully on the grace of God. The life of a Christian is one to be envied in life or in death. Jesus said, "I came that they might have life and have it more abundantly" (John 10:10).

We can never be at home in the midst of sin and evil, but we are called to be at home in the world that God has given us. When we work or play, when we sleep or sing, we are not taking time apart from the Christian life. Rather, we are *living* the Christian life. When we live fully, wholeheartedly, playfully, and danger-ously, we are fulfilling God's will for our lives. Our calling as Christians is to truly live. As St. Augustine said: "The glory of God is man truly alive."

No doubt some parts, perhaps most parts, of this book are frustrating. I have talked of patience and activity, work and rest, play and prayer, with scarcely a hint of how these might fit together. How on earth do we relate them all? I don't know, or at least I don't know in any sense that could be described as a set of rules and prescriptions.

NO "LITTLE BOOK OF INSTRUCTIONS"

Fortunately, it's not my goal to try and map out a full Christian life. I certainly couldn't, and I doubt very much whether anyone else could either. My goal is simpler. It is not to outline the "how to" of our lives but to suggest the *spirit* in which we called are to live. The simple and spiritual truth is that *this world is our home*, that our service in this world *is* service to God, that what we accomplish here we accomplish forever, that we await the resurrection of our bodies, that we expect a new heaven and an earth wherein God dwells in the midst of this creation, that we should live according to these beliefs.

We have rushed very rapidly through a survey of some aspects of our Christian calling. We have dealt in generalities, which is in escapable. But it is still central and crucial, though difficult, to have a sense of how these various dimensions of life fit together. The Bible is not at all explicit about this. It does not try to tell us how much rest or work or play we should have. It says nothing on auto repair. It is pretty quiet about universities. It doesn't lay out a political plan of action. It doesn't give environmental manifestos. It doesn't teach us everything, and so we can be biblically open to many possibilities life presents to us. Take work, for example.

It might be responsible to work on a job sixteen hours a day in order to meet a deadline, or to work at a job for only a few hours in order to free up time for evangelism or reflection.

It might be responsible to work for a high salary in order to give away to those in need, or to work at a subsistence wage because the work itself needs doing.

It might be responsible to devote most of our time to a paying job, or else to volunteer our time to do charitable work, serve the church, or nurture our families.

It might be responsible to excel in a profession, or to break out of a profession's self-interest and arrogance (Bernard Shaw, remember, once described a profession as "a conspiracy against the laity").

It might be responsible to search for tasks that are genuinely fulfilling and responsible, or to take up work that seems personally unfulfilling but helps others.

It might be responsible to take any job that will bring in the money we need, or it might be better to work in an existing organization or to start a new one.

This does not mean that our choices, if we have choices, are only relative or situational. There are guidelines we can find in the Scriptures. But our primary direction is not toward principles or rules but toward an honest response of faith shaped by a wise discerning of the spirits of the age. Rules channel faith; they are not substitutes for it.

The Bible does not, in the first place, give us a theory about our place in the world, or an ethics of work and rest, or a systematic theology of art or play or politics. What the Bible says about work, or politics, or anything else, it always says in relation to Jesus Christ; what we do is in relation to him, what he has done, and what he will do. The Scriptures don't try to answer all our questions but instead point us toward Jesus Christ with the promise that, through him, we can be reconciled to God. And so we can play, work, and rest. The integration point of our life is Jesus Christ, who says, "Come to me, all who labor, and I will give you rest. Take my yoke upon you" (Matt. 11:28–29).

Because of the nature of idolatry, we must beware of thinking that our Christian life simply presents a new set of goals or that it provides a blueprint for a new social order. Either of these can easily cause us to turn away from one idol in order to embrace another. New goals can easily become dominating forces to which everything else is subordinated and by which everything else is judged. As we've learned, an idol is a good thing in creation that we have made into a god. It becomes a "graven image," brutally carved in stone. As Christians, our response to God, which is what our entire life must be, should never *itself* be carved in stone.

CHILDREN OF THE HEAVENLY FATHER

Christian principles are not magic formulas. They do not always provide easy, clear, and simple solutions. They guide us in taking up our responsibility before God to care for God's world.

Rather than searching for *goals* to be achieved, we should try to understand *ways* to be followed. We must once again heed something to which we have referred many times—Jesus' admonition in the Sermon on the Mount:

> *Therefore I tell you, do not be anxious about*
> *your life, what you shall eat or what you shall drink*
> *nor about your body, what you shall put on. Is not*
> *life more than clothing? . . . But if God so clothes the*
> *grass of the field, which today is alive and tomorrow*
> *is thrown into the oven, will he not much more clothe*
> *you, you of little faith? . . . But seek first his*
> *kingdom and his righteousness, and all these things*
> *shall be yours as well. Therefore do not be anxious*
> *for tomorrow, for tomorrow will be anxious for itself.*
> *Let the day's own trouble be sufficient for the day.*
>
> Matthew 6:25–34

What Jesus says is demonstrated in the world about us. Our immediate future remains unrevealed. Despite the dreams of futurologists armed with computers, statistics, and projections, we simply do not know, and we cannot know, and we will not know what will happen in the future except in the final sense—and the only sense we need—that God will certainly bring all his purposes to completion. We are not capable of controlling or anticipating the outcome in any other way.

Our lives are not guaranteed of "success" as the world counts such things. It must not even be focused on success. Instead, we are called to take up a path of obedience to God as we face the problems confronting us, hour by hour, decade by decade. This doesn't mean we should abandon foresight or refuse to plan ahead. But it does mean that we cannot freeze the world into our mold or dictate a definite and certain future.

In preparing for the Lord's return, we are not to spend our time trying to calculate the date. Nor are we to sit around waiting for his appearance. Jesus himself said, "Of that day and hour no one knows" (Matt. 24:36). It was for doing this that Paul criticized the members of the Thessalonian church. They had stopped working and were idly waiting for Jesus' return (2 Thess. 3:6–13), even though Paul had already told them, "About times and dates . . . we do not need to write to you, for you know very well that the day of the Lord will come like a thief in the night" (1 Thess. 5:1, 2). We will not expect it: it will surprise us.

Jesus' parables emphasize the same themes. Focusing on the end of the age, he told of the five wise and the five foolish virgins. The wise took oil for their lamps while the foolish did not. When the bridegroom suddenly appeared, the foolish ones had neither oil nor the opportunity to buy any. Consequently, they were shut out of the banquet (see Matt. 25:1–12). Likewise, Jesus told his disciples, "Keep watch because you do not know the day or the hour" (Matt. 25:13). We keep watch, not because we know the time, but because we do not. Therefore we must always be ready by being about our Master's will in the world.

We are to await the Lord's return by being faithful in doing the things he has told us to do. The way to be ready for him is simply to be diligent about our Father's business. We are to pray, to hear and preach the Word, and to raise our children. We are to make a proper living, to be politically active, and to be responsible in every way until he comes. Martin Luther is reputed to have said, when asked what he would do if he knew the Lord would return tomorrow, "Plant a tree today."

When Jesus returns, we know that our work will be accepted not because we are perfect or have done such wonderful things but because, through Jesus Christ, we are accepted as God's children. Our works are not judged according to the standard of the law, but they are accepted in God's grace. Calvin writes of this with great power and beauty:

> *Those bound by the yoke of the law are like servants assigned certain tasks for each day by their masters. These servants think they have accomplished nothing, and dare not appear before their masters unless they have fulfilled the exact measure of their tasks. But children, who are more generously and candidly treated by their fathers, do not hesitate to offer them incomplete and half-done and even defective works, trusting that their obedience and readiness of mind will be accepted by their fathers, even though*

they have not quite achieved what their fathers intended. Such children ought we to be, firmly trusting that our service will be approved by our most merciful Father, however small, rude, and imperfect these may be.[2]

Therefore we pray and wait and work with hope. We need not fear the rejection of even our imperfect works. Instead we can confidently believe that God will accept and perfect them. He is our perfect Father, and he loves what his children struggle to do in faith.

A NEW HEAVEN AND EARTH

The biblical picture of a "new heaven and a new earth" can also help us to be neither overconfident nor despairing in our service. It is true that our task spans the entire creation. It is true that we will see a new heaven and a new earth. It is true that in Jesus Christ the power of sin has already been overcome. He said, "Be of good cheer, I have overcome the world" (John 16:33).

As we look at the world about us, we see people starving, yet we also see an increase in the means of feeding people. We see the development of weapons that can end the world, yet we see communications that can help unify the world. We live in a century that has perfected the art of genocide, yet it also proclaims a "Universal Declaration of Human Rights." Our world sways with the contradictory currents of God's preserving hand and humankind's repetitive evil.

When we consider the Church, we find the same contradictions holding sway. In a world afflicted with hunger, we have

Christian books on how to lose weight. We proclaim the Lord's justice, but in Serbia and South Africa, Christianity has become a byword for injustice and oppression. Preachers proclaim that Jesus Christ is the Lord of all creation but treat much of that creation as if it were alien to the gospel.

In this century we live in the greatest age of missionary expansion in the history of the Church. Despite our sins, the number of Christians increases vastly. The gospel spreads forth quickly over continents. But along with this expansion, we have suffered from inner contractions. The impact of Christianity has been lessening in the industrial lands of the North Atlantic and growing in the "third world." In this growth we can rejoice, for the fate of Christianity is now no longer tied to the fate of western culture. But we should also feel shame because the lessening is a sign that we have not seen the implications of the gospel in our own culture and nations. Our ability to lead our society in ways of blessing is sadly diminished.

This process is not irreversible. Christianity is the religion of new birth, new life, new beginnings. The hand of the Lord is not shortened, and it may stretch forth over us again. We have much to do. Our world suffers, waiting for the healing of Jesus Christ. We have, in and of ourselves, no strength or power. We kid ourselves if we pretend that we do or think that large numbers will carry the day. And, in an age that has produced the ongoing persecution of the church and the horrors of Auschwitz and Rwanda, all of our doings must be tinged with grief.

But, insofar as we hear the Word of God, insofar as we humbly and patiently seek to do God's will, then we can have hope. We have hope because God's promises will come to fruition, and we will see a new heaven and a new earth.

So, in this "between times," as we await the coming of the kingdom, we can fight evil, pain, and suffering in every part of life. Let us expect, and work toward, and pray for that day when at last the Voice cries:

Behold the dwelling of God is with them. He will dwell with them, and they shall be his people, and God himself will be with them; He will wipe away every tear from their eyes, and death shall be no more, neither shall there be mourning nor crying nor pain anymore, for the former things have passed away.

Revelation 21:3, 4

The kingdom of the world has become the kingdom of our Lord and of his Christ, and he shall reign forever and ever.

Revelation 11:15

Behold, I make all things new.

Revelation 21:5

N OTES

CHAPTER ONE

1. From the Latin, *nescius*, meaning ignorant. I take this information from an ad for the journal *Touchstone, First Things*, Jan. 1998, 40.

2. Dorothy L. Sayers, *Creed or Chaos?* (Manchester, N.H.: Sophia Institute Press, 1974), 6–7.

3. *Time* magazine reports that two-thirds of those who believe in heaven think only their soul goes there. March 31, 1997, 55.

CHAPTER TWO

1. See David Wells, *God in the Wasteland* (Grand Rapids, Mich.: Eerdmans, 1993), 37–44.

CHAPTER FOUR

1. 1 Cor. 8:6; 2 Cor. 5:16–19; Eph. 1:9–10, 15–23; 3:8–11; Phil. 2:9–11. See also John 3:16–17; Heb. 2:5–10; 2 Pet. 3:5–13.

CHAPTER FIVE

1. Quoted in Paul Althaus, *The Ethics of Martin Luther* (Philadelphia: Muhlenberg, 1972), 40–41. See also Paul Marshall, "Calling, Work and Rest," in M. Noll and D. Wells, *Christian Faith and Practice in the Modern World* (Grand Rapids, Mich.: Eerdmans, 1988), 199–217.

2. John Calvin, *Institutes*, IV.xx.16.

CHAPTER SIX

1. Calvin Seerveld. See acknowledgment reference.

2. See 1 Cor. 4:12; 15:10; 16:16; Eph. 4:28; Rom. 10:12; Gal. 4:11; Phil. 2:16; Col. 1:29; 1 Thess. 5:12.

3. See Eph. 4:17–32, esp. v. 28; 2 Cor. 11:9; 12:13; 1 Thess. 4:9–12; 2 Thess. 3:8; Acts 20:35.

4. See my *A Kind of Life Imposed on Man: Vocation and Social Order from Tyndale to Locke* (Toronto: University of Toronto Press, 1996), 14–18.

5. Sander Griffioen, "The Challenge of Marxist and Neo-Marxist Ideologies for Christian Scholarship," in *The Challenge of Marxist and Neo-Marxist Ideologies for Christian Scholarship*, ed. John Vanderstat (Sioux Center: Dordt College, 1982), 13.

6. John Paul II, *On Human Work (Laborem Exercens)* (Boston: St. Paul Editions, 1981), 61.

7. R. H. Tawney, *Religion and the Rise of Capitalism* (New York: Mentor, 1954), 233.

8. John Milton, *Paradise Lost*, IV: 610–20.

CHAPTER SEVEN

1. See Matt. 6:25–30; Josh. 24:2–13; Deut. 8:11–20; Luke 12:13–32.

2. W. E. Oates, "On Being a Workaholic (A Serious Jest)," *Pastoral Psychology* 19 (October 1968): 16–20.

3. Robert Banks and R. Paul Stevens, eds., *The Complete Book of Everyday Christianity* (Downer's Grove: InterVarsity Press, 1997), 313.

4. Thomas Aquinas, *Summa Theologia*, ii.2.9, 7.

5. Josef Pieper, *Leisure: The Basis of Culture* (New York: Random House, 1963), 40.

CHAPTER EIGHT

1. *Economist*, May 1, 1993.

2. Proverbs 8:30–31, translated by Cal Seerveld in his *Rainbows for the Fallen World* (Toronto: Tuppence Press, 1980), 53.

CHAPTER TEN

1. See Meredith G. Kline, "Oracular Origin of the State," in G. Tuttle, ed., *Biblical and New Eastern Studies* (Grand Rapids, Mich.: Eerdmans, 1978), 132–141; Paul Marshall, *Thine Is the Kingdom: A Biblical Perspective on Government and Politics Today* (Grand Rapids, Mich.: Eerdmans, 1986), 39–45.

2. Many people think that the Bible does not really contain "politics" but only a "theocracy" wherein God ruled directly. However, the term *theocracy*, literally meaning rule by God, is not found in the Bible. It was coined by Josephus, a first-century Jewish historian, to describe ancient Israel. He used it to emphasize God's *direct* involvement in Israelite affairs as distinct from the monarchies of other lands. However, Josephus also described *Moses* as Israel's "law-giver." He couldn't make up his mind whether God is merely the ultimate source of authority or if he directly wields that authority.

   This confusion of God as source and God as direct actor has plagued the term *theocracy* ever since. If the term is used to mean belief in God's *direct* acting, then it would seem to require something like God's continual appearance, or else a type of oracle, or else a human being claiming to give unmediated divine guidance. Examples of the first can perhaps be found in the Old Testament before the time of Noah (ending at Gen. 9:6). Examples of the third might be the claims of Pharaonic Egypt, imperial Rome, or imperial Japan.

As Jesus is really human and divine, the Church while he was on earth could perhaps have been called a genuine theocracy. This could also be the case when the Holy Spirit leads directly. But few people believe that this is the *only* form of rule, and most accept the need for some official structure for the political order. If theocracy is used in this narrow sense of God's *direct* action, there is nothing in the Christian faith that should lead Christians to be "theocrats" in the present age.

On the other hand, societies where the *ultimate* source of political authority is held to be God or God's law include many more than those usually described as "theocratic." God's sovereignty can be mediated or exercised by priests and kings, and also by judges, presidents, elected legislators, or the population itself. Many theories of democracy maintain that the people hold political authority, but they also believe that such authority has in turn been given to the people by God.

Similarly, many western constitutional democracies maintain that their laws reflect a higher divine or natural law. The American Declaration of Independence speaks of political authority ("rights") as being given by "Nature's God." The

Canadian constitution speaks of itself as founded on principles that recognize the "supremacy of God." Hence it is quite possible to be both a representative democracy and a so-called *theocracy*. Believing, as Christians should, that God is the source of political authority, can be quite compatible with what is generally, if somewhat loosely, called *democracy*.

3. One of the most astounding things about the modern world is how much Christianity contributes to the development of truly democratic societies. Nearly all free societies have a Christian cultural past. There are many complex reasons for this: we cannot simply say that Christianity immediately leads to democracy. Throughout Christian history there have been oppressions, wars, and dictatorships. Often Christians have been anything but open in their view of politics. But despite our sins and our shortsightedness, throughout all these tribulations, there seems to be something deeply within the Christian gospel that leads toward societies that respect and live the views of ordinary people. I believe that this is a reflection of God's call to each and every human being to take responsibility for the political order in which we live.

   Freedom House's 1998 survey, *Freedom in the World*, divides countries into "free," "partly free," and "unfree" societies. Of the eighty-one countries listed as free, seventy-four of them have a Christian cultural background. Of the others, two, Korea and Mauritius, have substantial Christian minorities (in December 1997, Korea switched from a Presbyterian to a Catholic president). Two, India and Japan, have political orders that were instituted by Britain and the United States, respectively. Another one is Israel. Another, Taiwan, currently has a Catholic president. The association of Christianity and democracy is one of the most solid correlations of political order in the world.

CHAPTER ELEVEN

1. See Mike Starkey, *Fashion and Style* (Crowborough: Monarch, 1995), 150.

2. Starkey, op. cit., 61; the following discussion draws much on Starkey.

3. Starkey, op. cit., 61–62.

4. Starkey, op. cit., 61.

5. On this see Calvin Seerveld, "Adornment" pp. 22–23 of Robert Banks and Paul Stevens, eds. *The Complete Book of Everyday Christianity* (Downer's Grove: InterVarsity Press, 1997).

6. Starkey, op. cit., 78–79.

7. Calvin Seerveld, *Rainbows for the Fallen World* (Toronto: Tuppence Press, 1980), 54–55.

CHAPTER THIRTEEN

1. On these see Celeste Schroeder, "Body," in *The Complete Book of Everyday Christianity* (Downer's Grove: InterVarsity Press, 1997), 77–80.

2. *The Book of Uncommon Prayer* (Dallas: Word, 1996), 61.

3. Bob Goudzwaard, *Aid for the Overdeveloped West* (Toronto: Wedge, 1975), 14–15.

4. Bob Goudzwaard, *Idols of Our Time* (Downer's Grove: Inter-Varsity Press, 1984). See also Herb Schlossberg, *Idols for Destruction* (Chicago: Regnery, 1990) and Tony Walters, *A Long Way from Home: A Sociological Exploration of Contemporary Idolatry* (Exeter: Paternoster, 1979).

5. Richard Mouw, interview, "The Life of Bondage in the Light of Grace," *Christianity Today*, December 9, 1988, 41, quoted in Cornelius Plantinga Jr., *Not the Way It's Supposed to Be* (Grand Rapids, Mich.: Eerdmans, 1996), 148. Plantinga's own discussion of addiction is helpful here.

6. I am not implying there are no sources of spiritual power in the world that act independently of human beings. There are such things as evil spirits. But I am suggesting that one major form of evil spiritual power exercised over us stems from the human act of idolatry itself. Perhaps there is even a continuum between idolatry and evil spirits. This is also an important theme in what is called "the theology of the powers."

7. Northrop Frye, "The Critical Path: An Essay on the Social Context of Literary Criticism," *Daedalus* (Spring, 1970): 268–342.

8. G. K. Chesterton, *Orthodoxy* (New York: Doubleday, 1924), 30–31.

CHAPTER FOURTEEN

1. C. S. Lewis, *God in the Dock* (Grand Rapids, Mich.: Eerdmans, 1964), 93.

2. Many Christians have problems with aspects of Spielberg's philosophy, but I thank God that he is not Michael Eisner of Disney, or Ted Turner of CNN. Spielberg seems to be a man with a strong moral compass and a concern for historical integrity. I hope Christians will some day produce better films than he has done, but we could certainly do worse.

3. Mike Starkey, *Fashion & Style* (Crowborough: Monarch, 1995), 19.

4. Dorothy L. Sayers, *Creed or Chaos?* (Manchester, N.H.: Sophia Institute Press, 1974), 24.

5. Sayers, op. cit. 25.

CHAPTER FIFTEEN

1. See Wim Rietkerk, *The Future Great Planet Earth* (Mussoorie, U.P. India: Good Books, 1989), 14ff. I read Rev. Rietkerk's book a week before finishing this and found many of the same themes expressed.

2. Søren Kierkegaard, "Patience," quoted in *The Book of Uncommon Prayer* (Dallas: Word, 1996), 93.

CHAPTER SIXTEEN

1. *Time*, March 31, 1997, 55.

2. John Updike, *Collected Poems* (New York: Alfred A. Knopf, 1993), 20–21.

3. See Al Walters, "Worldview and Textual Criticism in II Peter 3 v. 10," *Westminster Theological Journal*, vol. 49, 1987, 405–413. See also the Apostle Paul's discussion of the resurrection of the body, 1 Cor. 15:12–58, where he concludes "your labor in the Lord is not in vain."

4. A good discussion of many of these themes is given in Richard Mouw, *When the Kings Come Marching In: Isaiah and the New Jerusalem* (Grand Rapids, Mich.: Eerdmans, 1983).

CHAPTER SEVENTEEN

1. Paul Marshall, *Their Blood Cries Out* (Dallas: Word, 1997), 8.

2. John Calvin, *Institutes*, II. III. xix. 5.